The Food Repair Handbook

Michelle-Berriedale Johnson

The Food Repair Handbook

or how to rescue a disastrous dish

Macdonald

A **Macdonald** BOOK

© Michelle Berriedale-Johnson 1984

First published in Great Britain in 1984
by Macdonald & Co (Publishers) Ltd
London & Sydney

A member of BPCC plc

British Library Cataloguing in Publication Data
Berriedale-Johnson, Michelle
   The food repair handbook.
   1. Cookery
   I. Title
   641.5'028   TX651

   ISBN 0-356-10518-0

Phototypeset by Acorn Bookwork
Salisbury, Wilts.

Printed and bound in Great Britain by
Hazell, Watson & Viney Ltd
Aylesbury, Bucks.
A member of BPCC plc
Macdonald & Co (Publishers) Ltd
Maxwell House
74 Worship Street
London EC2A 2EN

Contents

Acknowledgements

With grateful thanks to my mother,
Patricia, Susie, Gillian, Lenore, Valerie,
Peggy, Dorothy, Christopher, Barry and
countless others who have generously
given of their disasters and partaken of
mine!

Introduction

If a disaster strikes, be it culinary or other, the worst thing you can do is to treat it as such . . . If you are alone, to do so is merely depressing, if other people are there, even if they are only family, they are made to feel awkward and uncomfortable. If guests are present and they are aware that the host or hostess is panicking and cannot cope, it can be acutely embarrassing for them and ruin an evening far more effectively than the culinary disaster that caused the panic.

Therefore, if faced with disaster, the first thing to do is to put on a brave face. This will make you feel better for a start. No matter what calamity has struck, there is a solution – even if it is only to confess to your disaster and have a good laugh. The fact that you do not get upset or distraught will make it easier for everyone else to make the best of an unpromising situation. Of course this is easy to say but less easy to achieve.

Two thoughts to bear in mind: if you are entertaining people who are older, more important, better cooks, wealthier, etc., than you and assuming that they are basically nice people, come clean and admit that you have had a disaster. They will probably remember an occasion on which something similar happened to them and will go out of their way to be helpful, sympathetic and generally civilized. If, on the other hand, you are older, more important, a better cook, wealthier, etc., than your guests, they will be thrilled and reassured that you can do stupid things and suffer the disasters which they thought were exclusively theirs.

If you do find yourself entertaining someone who is both important (husband's boss situation) and unsympathetic, unpleasant, or likely to revel in your discomfiture, you would do better to invent a mechanical reason (oven failure) for being unable to produce dinner and take them out to a restaurant – even if it does temporarily break the bank! Indeed, as an insurance if you do have to entertain such people and you are nervous about your own abilities, choose a restaurant and book a table. You can always cancel at the last minute.

The vast majority of culinary calamities though are retrievable. Or, if they cannot be rescued, provided you are wise and have laid in your stocks, you will be able to make last minute alterations or substitutions to the 'menu' that will be totally unnoticed by your guests.

Your success in fooling your guests will depend on two things: your skill in rescue or substitution and your 'brass neck'. If you have plenty of the latter you may get away with the most bizarre offerings. After all, if you can convince your guests that the blackened cinder they are breaking their teeth on is the most prized native dish of the Walawa-lawala tribe of the mid-Gobi desert, a great rarity sent to you at enormous expense, they can only feel flattered that you are prepared to share it with them. Getting away with this kind of thing depends on how well your guests know you, but, even if they do suspect, they can only admire your sang-froid and panache!

However, if you are somewhat more of a shrinking violet – or have pity on your guests and family – developing your skills as a rescuer and refurbisher of ruined meals might be more practical.

The first lesson to learn is when a dish is beyond recall. You do not want to waste valuable time on something that you will finally have to abandon. There are no golden rules in this department. Some simple disasters (like gluey mashed potatoes) are totally irretrievable, whereas what might appear at first sight to be past hope (a beef casserole whose beef has disintegrated), given a well-stocked cupboard, is easy to rectify.

If you are serious in your desire to repair, you will read this book *before* disaster strikes so that you will know, in most cases, what you can and what you cannot hope to rescue. If you are serious, you will also consult the lists of rescue materials that should always be kept in a disaster-prone cook's cupboard, you will find them on page 133. You would also be wise to consult the list of equipment which will assist you in your rescue mission. None of it is very expensive and it could save a tricky situation.

You will find that on page 133.

Remember too that it is no crime to serve commercially pre-prepared food. Much of what is sold today in speciality food shops is excellent quality, as well as being interesting and unusual. If you are really desperate for time or have managed to ruin the whole meal, judicious, if expensive, buying in a good delicatessen will provide you with a very acceptable meal. More practically though, the combination of a couple of 'bought' dishes with one or two home-made ones will relieve the strain on your nerves and your culinary self-confidence. A first class 'bought' pâté for example, with 'home-baked' bread out of the freezer, or exotic 'bought' ice cream with expensive dessert biscuits, combined with a home-made main course and vegetables would be excellent. You do not have to tell anyone and the chances are that they will never guess!

There are of course general disasters – such as the oven failing to work, falling over the cat and catapulting the roast into the dining room, or defrosting the wrong dish and not noticing till it is too late – that have nothing to do with cooking as such. Most of these are fairly comprehensive and will require substitution rather than repair work. I have provided a list of quick recipes that can be created out of your supplies, see page 130.

There are also genuine disasters such as fires, burns and bad cuts that can have far more serious consequences than a ruined dinner party.

You will find tips and advice on how to cope with both minor and more serious disasters in the first chapter.

Non-Culinary Disasters

Disasters happen to the best of us. Some can be looked back upon with laughter; others will be recalled with regret. However, the following sections will at least enable you to approach any disaster with a degree of cool confidence.

Human errors

Defrosting the wrong thing

It is all too easy with a large freezer to take out the wrong thing by mistake. Depending on what you actually did fish out, you can try brazening it out. For example, gooseberry fool, thinned down and heated up, could make an exotic fruit soup! But you might prefer to delve into the emergency rations cupboard.

Heating up canned foods

If you want to heat anything in its can, always ensure either that you have pierced the can to release the pressure or that you heat the can in boiling water. If the water boils dry and you have not pierced the can, the pressure in it will increase with the heat till it finally explodes, spraying the whole kitchen with its contents.

Running out of space

You can always bank pans up on top of each other, especially if their contents are already cooked and only need to be kept warm. Serving dishes and plates can be successfully warmed on top of cooking vegetables, etc.

Dropping things

Depending on what you drop and where you drop it, you may be able to scoop it back into its container and no one will be any the wiser. In the case of a cake, a slug of brandy or sherry will help to glue it together again. Alternatively, you may be able to cover the damage with some well-placed decorations. If you do fall over the cat and the joint lands under the table, all you can do is give everyone another drink and rush to the emergency supplies cupboard!

Not making enough of things

Depending on what you have not made enough of, you may be able to add more to it. A casserole can always have another frozen one added to it – even if it is not the same kind, it will make a much more interesting dish. You can serve an extra vegetable (tinned or frozen) to 'stretch' the meat. You can thin down a soup – or add a tin of something similar to it. You can add an extra course – a good tinned pâté and toast or some cheese and interesting biscuits after the dessert. Alternatively you can tell your guests that they are all too fat and should be on a diet!

Food 'going off'

Meat or fish that you suspect has gone off should be thrown out. It is simply not worth risking food poisoning because you are too mean to throw out the remains of the roast.

There is always a slight question mark over game, which needs to be hung to tenderize it. People who like really high game will eat a bird which is all but disintegrating. If they insist on doing so, they should at least take the precaution of eating it with a sharp fruit sauce or dressing to counteract the elderly meat.

Blue cheese presents the same problem. A Stilton under a microscope will reveal an apparently lethal dose of bugs and termites at work. Yet a mature Stilton is the *pièce de résistance* of many a Christmas table.

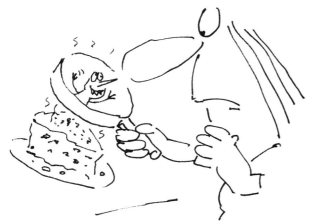

Some stomachs can stand more in the way of 'powerful' food than others. You will find that your body will be a good guide. If you are nauseated by the smell or thought of eating something, there is a good chance that your stomach could not cope with it. Yet the same tender morsel might smell wonderful to someone with an iron-clad stomach which would be totally unperturbed by it.

Vegetables and fruit normally go soft and mushy as they get old. Old vegetables and fruits lose their nutrients and their flavour but they will seldom harm you. Should one harbour an insect you would be wise to throw it out.

Cooked dishes, soups, stocks, casseroles, etc., that have gone off will let you know all about it. They will smell appalling and heave and bubble at you. The only place for them is down the toilet or the waste-disposal unit. A couple of lemons ground down the waste-disposal afterwards will get rid of most of the smell.

Power and gadget failures

Power failure

Since the arrival of natural gas, gas seldom fails; electric power disappears far more often.

A calor gas stove or a fondue set could achieve hot soup at least. Clever, if precarious, piling of dish upon dish, on top of the calor stove, could achieve several hot dishes, but you might be wise to stick to one and plenty of wine to warm the inner man!

Oven

It is possible to cook virtually anything that should be cooked in an oven on top of a stove.
A chicken for roasting could be casserole or pot roasted – see page 98.
A soufflé could be turned into a timbale – see page 40.
Roast potatoes could be replaced by sauté potatoes.

This is fine, provided that you have known from the start that your oven was not working. However, if you get home and discover that the automatic timer has failed to turn the oven on and you only have half an hour before the guests arrive, then you will have to abandon whatever you had planned and choose a dish from your instant supplies cupboard.

Microwaves

Microwave ovens must be regularly checked by a qualified person to make sure that the seals are intact. It *very* rarely happens, but should the seal break and radiation leak out it could cause all kinds of nasties like cancer and sterility.

Anything that can be cooked in a microwave can also be cooked in something else but it will take longer. However, inexperienced users of microwaves are liable to overcook their dishes. If you do so, they will be quite irretrievable – either rock hard or totally incinerated.

Freezers

If your freezer goes off because of a power cut or because it breaks down you have about three days' grace with a chest freezer, and two and a half with an upright – as long as you do not open the thing. With a chest freezer, every time you open it you will lose about half an hour of frozen time; with an upright freezer you will lose anything from 1-1½ hours at each opening.

Fridges

Loss of temperature with an ordinary fridge is more immediate. Without opening, the food will last up to 12 hours only and every time you open it you will lose another half an hour. If it is winter, transfer everything to a larder, put it on a windowsill or even in the garden covered with large saucepans or bowls to protect it from marauders. If it is summer, you will just have to eat the contents of the fridge as fast as you can and buy for each day, or, if it is really hot, for each meal.

If you actually needed the fridge to chill what you were preparing you could go out and buy some ice and use that, but it would be much easier to change the menu.

Pressure cookers

Pressure cookers are safe and useful pieces of equipment as long as they are properly used. NEVER open the pressure release valve when the cooker is up to pressure as it will release a jet of superheated steam, which can scald badly.

NEVER attempt to remove the top of a pressure cooker until the whole thing has been cooled under running water. If you did manage to open it before it had cooled, the build up of pressure inside would blow the lid off with lethal force.

Non-functioning electrical gadgets

1 If your electric cooker fails, do not attempt to discover what is wrong with it yourself. Call the maintenance engineer.

2 If any of your normal electrical appliances fail to work:
a) turn off the socket and pull out the plug
b) open the plug and check the fuse
c) make sure that all the naked wires are firmly in their holes and that the screws that hold them in place are tightly screwed up.

All too many electrical appliances have carelessly fitted plugs with wires 'floating around' in their holders. This causes arcing which creates heat which, if allowed to continue for long enough, could cause the fuse to blow or the plug to catch fire.

3 If the appliance still does not work, call the maintenance engineer.

Fires and explosions

Gas

Any suspicion of a gas leak should be reported at once, even though natural gas is not poisonous. If leaking gas is trapped in an enclosed area, contact with a spark will cause it to explode. For example, if there was a gas leak into your self-lighting oven, when you turned the oven on it would ignite an oven full of gas. Gas explosions of this kind have been known to wreck whole houses.

Electricity

Electrical fires seldom happen in the kitchen but should one occur:

1 Turn off the mains supply.

2 Smother the fire with a fire blanket, if you have one, or anything that is both DRY and *NOT* MAN MADE FIBRE.

3 AFTER THE MAINS ARE SWITCHED OFF, use water to douse the fire.

Hot oil

Most kitchen fires are caused by hot oil catching light. If oil gets too hot, it will spontaneously ignite. In other words, if you put the chip pan on and forget it while you answer the phone or go to make the beds, once the fat gets hot enough it will catch fire of its own accord.

The oil can also ignite if it comes in contact with direct heat. This usually happens if you attempt to cook too much at once causing the oil to bubble up and overflow out of the pan onto the flame. Always deep-fry in a large pan with plenty of space for the oil to bubble up in.

If your oil does catch light:

1 DO NOT ATTEMPT TO MOVE IT.

2 TURN OFF THE HEAT.

3 COVER THE PAN. You can use a lid or metal tray if you have one near. Alternatively, use a fire blanket or a WET TEA CLOTH. Cover the pan carefully, keeping the cloth or blanket between your hands and the pan so as not to burn your hands. The idea is to exclude the oxygen that is essential for the fire to burn.

DO NOT attempt to put the fire out with WATER. The oil is so hot that it will only vaporize or turn into steam immediately, which will fail to put out the fire and probably burn you.

Unless you are going to regularly maintain it, do not bother to keep a fire extinguisher. Without regular maintenance they cannot be relied on and may fail you in time of need. A small fire blanket is much more useful, easier to store and simpler to use.

First aid

Burns and scalds

The more extensive the burn, the more dangerous it is, even if it is not very deep. The most important thing is to reduce the temperature in the burnt area. Place it carefully either in cool water or under gently running cool water and keep it there for at least 10 minutes.

If it is a bad burn that may cause swelling, try to remove anything constrictive like rings, bangles or boots before the swelling starts and makes it impossible to get them off.

If the person's clothes have been soaked in boiling water, they should be carefully removed. If they have been dry burnt, they should be left alone as they will have been sterilized by the heat.

For chemical burns by corrosives such as kettle descalers, remove the clothes carefully and wash the area as thoroughly as possible under gently running cool water both to reduce the temperature and to wash away any remains of the chemical.

If you are at all worried about the seriousness or extent of the burn (a burn that covers over 10 per cent of the body surface – a leg or the chest – can be fatal and the person *must* be treated in hospital), call an ambulance or get the person to a hospital. Meanwhile, treat him for shock by laying him down and covering him with a light blanket. Cover the burnt area with a light, dry dressing. Give the person small cold drinks at frequent intervals and plenty of reassurance and comfort.

Do not try to apply any kind of ointments or treatment and, if the person is cold, do not try to 'warm him up' with hot water bottles or more blankets. You will only draw the blood to the skin and away from the vital organs where it is needed.

If it is a relatively minor but painful burn, run it under cold water as for a more serious one. Then either apply a dressing of bicarbonate of soda mixed with water into a paste and hold lightly in place with a bandage, or cover the area with a non-adhesive sterile dressing and hold it in place with a bandage. Alternatively, use a paraffin gauze dressing held in place with a light bandage. If the burn blisters, try not to break the blister any sooner than you can help, as it is protecting the wound.

Burns or scalds of the mouth or throat

These normally only happen with children who try to drink out of the spout of a boiling kettle. This can be VERY SERIOUS. Take them immediately to hospital or call an ambulance. While waiting, lay them down on their sides and give them small sips of cold water to drink.

Cuts

Kitchen cuts are usually of the incision or the puncture kind. In other words one cuts the flesh cleanly, or relatively cleanly with a knife or tin edge, or one punctures a hole in oneself with a skewer or tin opener.

The puncture kind of cut can be more

dangerous as it is deep and does not bleed freely, so that there is a greater chance of infection. Unless you are absolutely sure that the cut is clean, it would be wise to get it medically checked.

For an incision cut the main thing to ensure is that it is clean. Incision cuts usually bleed profusely thereby cleaning themselves, but put the wound under running water and allow it to bleed freely for a couple of minutes to ensure that all possible dirt is removed. Then attempt to stop the bleeding.

The best way is to press a pad of lint, cotton wool or even tissues or clean paper towel over the wound and, if possible, raise the injured part so as to discourage the flow of blood. If it was a large gash, try to press the two sides together under the pad. If it bleeds through, cover it with another pad and apply gentle but firm pressure until it stops bleeding. Then gently remove the temporary dressing and apply a new clean one, which can be held in place either with an adhesive or tied bandage.

Although the wound will heal quicker if left uncovered (once the blood has clotted and it has stopped bleeding), the chances are that you will knock it and dislodge the scab thus delaying healing, so, unless you can be sure that you will look after your cut, cover it with a clean bandage.

If you are using the finger or hand that has been cut, change the dressing or bandage fairly frequently, as it will get both dirty and wet – neither of which will help the poor thing to heal.

If the wound is large and the bleeding profuse, do your best to staunch the flow of blood and get medical help as soon as possible.

Salmonella poisoning

Salmonella poisoning, in its early stages, is almost indistinguishable from ordinary poisoning: nausea, vomiting and diarrhoea. However, if salmonella poisoning is suspected, immediately contact your doctor.

Soups

In most households, disasters, rather like Cinderella's pumpkin, get turned into soups rather than soups undergoing their own transformations. On the whole, soups are remarkably forgiving, although there are still fertile areas for the conscientiously disaster-prone cook. But, since most soups are prepared in advance, you do at least have time for repair work. Moreover, the disasters do not tend to be of a cataclysmic nature, so rescue operations are relatively simple.

Disastrous soups usually suffer from one of three defects: no flavour; too much salt; or curdled or separated texture. (There are, of course, other minor hazards like failing to make enough in the first place, forgetting the soup is simmering and reducing it to a mud cake in the bottom of the pan, or even taking what you think to be delicious cream of chicken soup out of the freezer only to discover, too late, that it is gooseberry fool. For emergency measures in these cases, see pages 23 and 9). Cures vary according to the type of soup but if all else fails, distraction is the name of the game.

Distraction techniques

Keep some really nice croûtons in the deep freeze – you could 'devil' them by sprinkling them with a little cayenne pepper when they are cooked. Make sure they are really hot and crisp (10 minutes in a hot oven should achieve that) and dump great handfuls in the middle of each dish. The guests will be so fascinated by the croûtons that they will quite forget to notice the soup. The same principle can be applied with whipped cream, handfuls of chopped parsley or chopped fresh mint – if you can get it, or spoonfuls of aioli (a type of mayonnaise heavily flavoured with garlic) if you are dealing with a fish soup. The combination of the cream with a few sunflower seeds, a pinch of paprika, parsley or chives, even some toasted chopped or flaked almonds, will have an even more distracting effect.

As a secondary line of defence, serve the soup with really hot and pungent garlic bread or some outlandish new crackers, rolls or bread. Invent a story about their origin or the fight the baker and his wife were having when you bought them, etc., etc., so that your guests will have finished the soup (and failed to notice what it tasted like) by the time you have finished the story.

However, assuming that you have time to rectify the original problem, here are some real culinary cures.

Vegetable soups

These fall into the thick and thin categories. The thin soups are the ones that still have the bits of the relevant vegetables floating around; the thick ones are those that have been liquidized, puréed or blended.

Lack of flavour

The most common problem with vegetable soups is lack of flavour. This nearly always comes from insufficient cooking of the vegetables in the early stages. Excellent vegetable soups can be made with water alone as long as the vegetables have been fried and sweated very thoroughly before the liquid is added. The flavour is greatly improved if butter or a good quality oil is used for the frying and sweating.

Even if the early cooking has been skimped, all is not lost. A small piece of stock cube always gives flavour, as does a splash of medium sweet sherry. If it is appropriate to the vegetables, a spoonful of tomato purée will help, as will an ex-

tra nob of butter. A concentrated packet or tin of the same variety of soup will also add flavour. If it is a packet, take care that you add the soup to the packet and not the packet to the soup – otherwise you will not only have flavourless soup but lumpy flavourless soup. Depending on the vegetables concerned, soya sauce, Worcestershire sauce, even curry paste (or curry powder that has been fried in a little butter first) are all good flavour enhancers. Salt and pepper are essential, of course, but should *not* be overdone.

If you are still not happy with the flavour of the soup, liquidizing or blending it may help, as this will crush all the ingredients, letting out any flavour that might lurk within. If the flavours in the soup are rather badly amalgamated through lack of early cooking, it will also help to blend them together.

Of course, the enthusiast may go to the other extreme and fry the vegetables so well that they are reduced to blackened cinders. If they are totally charred, they are irretrievable and must go out. However, if they merely have a coating of charcoal, go ahead and add the stock –

if the soup is cooked long and slowly, the burnt taste will convert itself into 'deep' flavour.

It is always better to use a freshly-made stock than water or a tin or cube of stock. However, beware of ham stock, as it has a horrible habit of turning itself into brine when you are not looking.

Overseasoning

Seasoning should be added with care, especially in the early stages. The more the soup cooks, the more concentrated the flavour will become, which means that if you add a lot of salt at the beginning in the hopes of creating flavour you will end up with Dead Sea Soup. If this happens, potatoes, white bread-crumbs, cream and parsley can all be used to 'mop up' the saltiness. The soup should always be liquidized so that the 'mopping' agent has the best chance to percolate throughout.

Garlic can also be overdone. If you ever want your friends to speak to you again, parsley is the best antidote, although potatoes and breadcrumbs are quite effective.

Adding 'body'

Potatoes and brown breadcrumbs (white are very flavourless) are also good ways of thickening a thin vegetable soup – giving it 'body' for a cold winter's day. Caution, though, is advised with pota-toes. Waxy new potatoes can be very glutinous, and the end result could be closer to a fondue than a soup! If you want to thicken a 'bitty' soup, rice and pulses, either tinned or freshly cooked, work well.

Meat soups

Very much the same problems and cures apply to meat soups as to vegetable ones.

Flavouring

If you are doing the job properly and using bones and meat for the basis, you should pre-bake or fry the bones – it does help bring out the flavour. How-ever, for meat soups it is the cooking in the liquid rather than the early frying that is particularly important and this step cannot be speeded up. If you have not cooked the meat long enough in the liq-uid, you will have to add flavour with a chicken or beef stock cube, an extra tin or packet of the same soup, butter, or red wine, white wine or sherry, depending on the meat. Certain spices can also help –

ginger with chicken for example, or chilli or curry powder with beef. Cook them very lightly in a little butter before adding them to the soup to avoid that horrible raw spice taste, and then simmer the soup for 5–10 minutes to let the flavour come out.

Padding out

Certain last minute vegetables are also good disguisers of deficiencies. Tinned sweet corn, asparagus tips or palm hearts, if you can afford them, in a chicken soup; tinned tomatoes, frozen peas or chopped beans in a 'hearty' meat soup. Some almost raw vegetables also work well: very thinly sliced Chinese leaves, julienned carrots or turnips just simmered in the soup for a couple of minutes before it is served. These can add texture as well as interest to an otherwise boring soup. If you really want to jolt your guests into failing to notice the basic boringness of the soup, you could always add something outlandish like some finely sliced, presoftened prunes to a chicken soup, or a tin of cherries to a beef soup – or some dried seaweed from a packet to almost anything.

Over- and under-cooking

If the meat and/or vegetables have managed to burn themselves in the early cooking, the addition of curry powder will disguise the burnt taste – although the latter will often disappear anyhow if you simmer the soup for long enough. If the meat or vegetables did not get

cooked long enough at either stage, the soup (assuming that it is a dark soup) will probably look rather pale and insipid. You can add commercial colouring, but a little caramelized sugar works as well and adds something in terms of flavour.

Flour- and egg-thickened soups

Both vegetable and meat soups are often thickened either with flour or a liaison of eggs. The former is relatively safe, the latter hazardous for disaster-prone soup makers.

Thickening with flour

This is simple provided that you always add small amounts of soup to the flour till you have a thick paste and then add the paste to the soup. If you just throw the flour in, you will inevitably end up with golf balls of raw flour floating in the soup. If the soup is a thin one, there is no problem: just put it through a sieve, thereby eliminating the lumps. However, if it is the kind of soup that already has 'bits' in it (for instance, a mushroom soup made with sliced rather than puréed mushrooms), you cannot sieve it without losing the 'bits'. In this case, cook the soup thoroughly so that at least the floury lumps are cooked floury lumps, then add cooked white rice, barley, or even small pieces of pasta, which can mingle with the floury lumps and put even the most discerning guest off the trail.

Another way to avoid lumps is to add your flour to the vegetables *before* the liquid (rather than after) and cook it for a couple of minutes (as for a white or brown roux). There is always the danger of forgetting it at this stage and letting the flour burn. If it is totally charred, it will have to go out, but, if it is only a charred outer layer, continue as planned. If you end up with little black bits floating in the soup, be sure to add your pepper *very* coarsely ground, so that once again the guests will be confused. Alternatively, add some toasted sunflower or sesame seeds, or even crushed almonds before serving, which will have the same effect.

An overdose of flour can also make for a very stodgy soup. The only cure for this is to thin it with water, milk, wine and water mixed (but not too much wine or it will be very acid), or stock. The problem with most of these is that they will dilute or alter the flavour of the soup and you will have to start again on improving it.

Egg-thickened soups

These come in the luxury end of the trade and their main disadvantage is that, if allowed to boil, they inevitably curdle. As with flour, the egg (yolk or whole) should be mixed with a small quantity of the warm soup, then added to the main body and heated gently to allow the thickening to take place. If it boils, it will curdle rather than thicken.

If the egg curdles, you have several options. You can brave it out and pretend you meant it to be that way all along. After all, some of the most famous Italian, Greek and Chinese soups are made by whisking egg into a thin soup to create strands of cooked egg. All that happens when the egg curdles is that it cooks too much and too fast to act as a thickening agent and turns itself into scrambled egg instead. Alternatively, if it is a thin or puréed soup, you can sieve it to remove the bits of egg, or you can blend it, which merely purées the bits of egg. In the latter case, you may have to sacrifice whatever other 'bits' you have in the soup.

Pulse soups

Pulse soups are normally vegetable or meat soups that use a pulse (lentil, bean, etc.) as the bulk element. They are relatively hazard-free as long as you remember to soak the pulse first if it needs it. You will only learn this from the packet, as some dried beans and peas can be cooked straight from the packet whereas others (most haricot or butter beans, for example) need many hours of soaking if they are not to remain like bullets. To get a really tasty soup it is best to use a well-flavoured stock – although herbs and bits of bacon can add to the flavour. Do not salt until you are well into the process and the pulse is nearly cooked. If you salt earlier, the salt will react with the pulse to create atomic-bomb-proof bullets that nothing will ever soften.

Some bean soups tend to separate, especially when you blend them. In this case, add a small amount of flour-and-stock paste to bind them together.

Fish soups

Fish soups have a possibly natural tendency to taste watery. Therefore you need to make the stock properly to extract the maximum flavour. Cook the fish bones and skin hard and rapidly with plenty of vegetables and some wine for optimum effect.

If you use white or flat fish, this has a nasty habit of disintegrating, so it is always wise to keep some frozen prawns, potted shrimps, or even a tin of tuna fish or salmon, as a last minute additive if all the rest of the fish has apparently swum away.

Potted shrimps are also excellent for adding flavour, as they are preserved in well-spiced butter. White wine is a good flavour enhancer too, but take care, as too much can taste very acid.

Any kind of fish in its shell looks impressive, even though it may not taste of much – if it has been frozen, for example. Most shellfish (mussels, clams, etc.) can be bought frozen or tinned in their shells and are invaluable as a last minute 'upgrader'. Of course, the soup will taste infinitely better if you grit your teeth and use fresh shellfish in the first place. If you do so, do make sure that they are alive. When you throw them into the hot soup they should all open up – throw out any that do not. You can-

not be blamed for feeding someone a bad bit of shellfish – it can happen in the classiest of restaurants – but, unless you thoroughly dislike your guests, shellfish poisoning is not a fate you would wish on them.

Aioli is another excellent disguise for a flavourless fish soup – especially if you serve lots of hot bread with it. If you're desperate, you can make aioli with bought mayonnaise (*not* salad cream) mixed with several crushed cloves of garlic, although home-made is better.

Clear soups

Clear soups are for the cook with time and patience to spare. However, they are not difficult, *provided* you follow the recipe.

Clarifying

The main thing is to skim off all the debris, both in the early stages when you are bringing the stock to the boil (and the scum needs to be removed) and in the later stage when using egg white and shell to clear the soup. If it does not clear the first time you add the egg white and shell, the only answer is to go on repeating the performance until it does, taking great care not to break the skin that the egg white should produce on the top of the soup. No amount of sieving through muslin or jelly bags will ever achieve the crystal clarity of the five-star consommé.

However, if repeated applications of egg fail to achieve this desirable result, then a touch of lateral thinking is required. A large dollop of soured cream with some lumpfish roe or caviar on top, or a heavy splattering of chopped parsley, chives or ham will mingle with your muddy soup and render its lack of clarity invisible to the public.

Adding flavour

If, on the other hand, you have managed to achieve a clear but flavourless soup, that is easier to deal with. Sherry, Madeira, port (if desperate), lemon juice or tinned consommé all provide excellent flavour boosters. If all else fails, chill the soup well, chop it and serve it on crushed ice with Melba toast. Your guests will be so impressed with the presentation of your soup that they will be oblivious to its lack of flavour.

If it fails to gel and you have time, just add some gelatine – approximately half the amount you would normally add, i.e. ¼ oz/5 g per pint/600 ml/ 2½ cups rather than ½ oz/10–15 g. If you do not have time for this, serve it as a 'soft' consommé: 'It brings the flavour out so much better than when it is totally chilled, you know . . .'

Cold soups

Cold soups are almost foolproof and very rewarding. The simplest ones are usually made of puréed vegetables of one kind or another. Remember that chilling dulls the flavour, so if the soup is to taste at all when it is chilled, it must taste reasonably powerful when it is hot. You should also remember that liquids tend to thicken as they cool, so a thick hot soup may turn into a cold congealed mass. You can thin the soup when it is cold but it is more difficult to adjust the flavour, as the seasonings do not get absorbed as easily as when it is hot.

Garnishing

Cold soups are easy to garnish 'inspiredly'. Most raw salad vegetables, finely chopped, add texture, flavour and colour: celery, parsley, chives, peppers, watercress, fresh herbs or whatever the garden offers. Alternatively, chopped hard-boiled eggs, olives, raw ham, anchovies, sesame seeds or nuts will do equally well. In almost all circumstances the addition of double cream, chopped parsley and fresh lemon juice will be an improvement.

General points

Freezing

Most soups freeze well (with the exception of consommé, which loses its gelatinous quality), but they may become rather bitty or separated when they defrost. If this happens, just blend them for a few minutes in a liquidizer or food processor.

Wine

Wine nearly always improves a soup. However, it does tend to emphasize saltiness, so, if this is already a problem, do not add wine.

Wine always needs to be cooked – raw wine in a cooked dish is not a good idea. It can also curdle soups with a heavy milk content. If this happens, continue to cook, as it will often sort itself out. If not, add a little double cream, which will normally bind it. If all else fails, put it in the blender.

Failing to make enough

A judicious addition of the main liquid ingredient will usually stretch a soup to cover the number required unless you have really badly underestimated. In this case, you may need a few extra 'flavour enhancers' to make up for the additional liquid. If you have really only provided enough for half a spoonful each, then you will have to have recourse to the packet or tin. In this case, bring in the full range of 'distraction techniques'.

Letting it boil away

You can at least be sure that the basis for your soup will have flavour, although it may not be exactly what you, or the recipe, had in mind. Slowly add first water, then stock or milk, depending on what you had originally intended the soup to be. Stir continuously to avoid lumps, but try to avoid scraping all the burnt bits off the bottom of the saucepan. Keep adding the liquid until it reaches a manageable consistency. At this stage you can either be brave and claim to have discovered a new and exciting recipe using exotic spices and ingredients, *very* difficult to obtain, or you can add the more normal range of cream, sherries, wines and parsley. These should render it acceptable if not necessarily riveting.

Making very large quantities

Large quantities of any hot food, if left to cool very slowly, have a horrible habit of going off. There are few things less attractive than a heaving pot of soup, quite apart from the problem of what you are going to feed to the descending hordes! Onions and green peas are particularly unfriendly in this matter, so do take care, as there is *nothing* you can do with a pot of evil smelling soup except flush it down the toilet. If you are at all worried, split the hot soup into several small containers and chill it well in these.

Sauces

Sauces should never be left to their own devices. Almost without exception, if ignored, they will curdle, burn, go lumpy, go thin, boil away to nothing or splatter themselves all over the kitchen out of sheer malice. Even when lovingly tended, they are quite capable of ruining themselves while you just answer the phone or dash to the toilet. With this in mind, the disaster-prone cook would be well advised to leave the touchier members of the family (Hollandaise, mayonnaise and custard) well alone and to approach even its less neurotic members with caution.

Having said this, there are, of course, certain sauces that are quite difficult to destroy. The juices that run from the roast, for example, are unequalled as a sauce for the meat and require nothing from the cook at all – although it is possible to leave the meat in the oven so long

that the juices dry up. If you commit this crime, pour a little wine, water or stock into the roasting tin over a low heat and stir it well. The liquid will gradually dislodge the burnt bits from the pan and turn them into a, hopefully, delicious gravy. Our grandfathers had even easier cures – just a little warmed port poured over their roast meat. It may be a bit powerful for modern tastes, but it is certainly very simple. Would that the modern cook's range of sauces were as uncomplicated!

Gravies

Gravies are among the simplest of sauces – which does not prevent them from going wrong! They depend for their flavour on the juices that come from the meat and that can, all too easily, burn in the roasting tin. It helps if the tin is greased before the meat goes in. Most meats lose a lot of fat in the cooking, and it is important to remove the excess fat before you try to make the gravy. If you cannot come to terms with pouring it out of the pan – roasting tins have a nasty habit of slipping from the hand and cascading their contents all over your feet – use a bulb skimmer to suck up the juices from under the fat. Alternatively, pour

the fat and juices into a separator gravy boat with two spouts, one running from the juicy bottom and one from the fatty top. If you fail to remove the fat, it will be impossible to make edible gravy, as you will need a quite disproportionate amount of flour to absorb the fat. You would do better to abandon it and resort to the warmed port.

A simple addition of stock, wine or sherry and seasoning to the de-fatted juices will make an excellent sauce but it will be very thin. If you want it thicker, add a little flour to the roasting tin – normally a tablespoonful will be quite enough for a standard size roast. You will need to stir the roux continuously if it is to brown without burning, as the tin will cover a much larger area than the burner. If you fail to get it brown enough, gravy browning or a little caramel will improve the colour greatly.

Taste the gravy before you season it and season with discretion, as the pan juices could be very salty, especially if they have already been reduced. If you oversalt, dilute with stock or water (not wine, as it tends to emphasize saltiness) and add some chopped parsley to absorb the salt. If the gravy is tasteless, a little redcurrant jelly will give flavour, as will a small piece of stock cube, butter, or a tablespoon of sweet or medium sherry.

Flour-based sauces

Flour-based sauces are the brown and white roux on which every cookery student spends his first week; what are known in books of French *haute cuisine* as the '*sauces mères*'. The principles for both brown and white sauces are exactly the same, the difference lying only in the fact that for a brown sauce one browns the roux, for a white sauce one, hopefully, does not.

Method

There are three golden rules for making flour-based sauces and if you stick to them you should not have any problems.

1 Always measure the ingredients exactly.

2 Make sure the flour is cooked before you add the liquid.

3 Add the liquid gradually.

The proportions for a sauce the consistency of cream are 1 oz/25 g butter to 1 oz/25 g flour to ½ pint/300 ml/1¼ cups of liquid. The butter should always be melted before you add the flour and, when you add the flour, you should stir it well to make sure that it amalgamates properly. The roux should then be cooked gently for a couple of minutes without turning colour for a white sauce, longer and until it is coloured for a brown. If it is cooked over too high a heat, the starch in the flour will shrink, which will prevent it from thickening properly. If it is not cooked enough, it will not absorb the liquid evenly and you will get a lumpy sauce. A warm liquid will amalgamate more easily with the flour, but a hot liquid will react on the flour, causing a granular texture that nothing will get rid of it. Add the liquid gradually and keep stirring; if you do this, the sauce should remain lump-free from the start. However, if lumps do form, don't worry; if you go on stirring and cooking gently, they will normally get bored and go away. If, despite your greatest care, you still end up with lumpy sauce, you can always put it through a sieve.

Over- or under-cooking

If you are making espagnole or any of the vegetable-based brown sauces, lumps are irrelevant, as the sauce will be strained anyhow. With these sauces, you are more likely to burn the vegetables and roux in an attempt to get them well browned and flavoursome than anything else. If you do burn them, ignore the burnt bits and soldier on. If the sauce refuses to thicken properly because you burnt the roux, reduce it by simmering it gently – you may have slightly less sauce but it will taste delicious! If, even after you have sieved it, you still have little bits of burnt something-or-other floating in your sauce, be sure to grate your pepper coarsely so that all the black flecks look like pepper!

BEFORE   PEPPER   AFTER

If the sauce has a floury taste, that is because it is not sufficiently cooked; continue to simmer till the taste disappears.

Consistency

If, for whatever reason, your sauce is still too thin, thicken it with a little cornflour – mix this to a paste in a bowl with some of the warm sauce before adding. Or you could use some *beurre manié* – equal quantities of soft butter and flour beaten very well together and added to the sauce in little walnuts. *Beurre manié* gives a better flavour but can curdle.

Alternatively, your sauce may be too thick. In this case, you need only thin it with more of whatever liquid you have been using. Do not add too much wine, especially if you have already seasoned the sauce, as it will make it too salty.

Removing fat

If the sauce is greasy or has a layer of butter or fat floating on the top, soak it up with sheets of paper towel just laid over the sauce. The paper will absorb the fat, leaving the sauce behind. Alternatively, chill the sauce. This will congeal the fat, which can then be scraped off with a spoon.

Adding flavour

If your sauce is smooth but flavourless, have recourse to the stock cube, Worcestershire sauce, sherry or port bottle, or the redcurrant jelly pot – provided it is a brown sauce. A lump of butter will help both a brown and a white sauce but take care not to add too much or to boil the sauce after you have added the butter, as it could curdle.

Egg yolks also add flavour but they are even more liable to curdle. If you do decide to try one, beat it with a little cold water before adding it to the sauce and do not let the sauce boil after you have added it.

Cheese sauce

This can be both the most delicious and the most truly awful of the flour-based sauces. A good cheese sauce must be based on a good white sauce, not a lumpy mess of flour and water. It also requires well-flavoured cheese with a good texture. Soapy cheeses lose their flavour when cooked and have a nasty habit of going stringy. Swiss Gruyère, in particular, should be used only by the expert, as a rope of sauce is impossible to deal with and unrescuable. If your sauce is flavourless, a spoonful of good mustard will do wonders for it.

Remember that sauces are intended to complement the food, not to drown it so, unless you have a singularly boring and tasteless dish, do not make the sauce too much of a knock-out.

Egg-based sauces

There can be no doubt that Hollandaise and its derivatives (Béarnaise, Maltaise, etc.) are the *prima donnas* of the sauce world. If they do not get constant and unremitting attention from the cook, they will always become temperamental and curdle. They are even sensitive to weather conditions, and in humid or thundery weather are liable to throw a tantrum no matter what you do. The vital thing, as with all egg-based sauces, is to prevent the mixture boiling and turning the egg into a close approximation of breakfast.

Always make Hollandaise in a double saucepan (thus reducing the chance of boiling) and always cook it slowly. A sudden blast of heat, even if it does not curdle the sauce, will make the eggs granular. Add the butter slowly and stir continuously. If you want to make the sauce before you need it and keep it warm, do so only on the lowest of heats or over a saucepan of lukewarm water – be careful as, if it does fall apart, you will not have time to do much about it.

Curdling

However, if the worst happens and the sauce does curdle you have several options. Take the pan immediately off the heat and plunge it into a bowl of cold water – this will often bring the sauce back. Alternatively, take it off the heat and stir in a tablespoonful of cold water or cream. If the sauce goes altogether, you can usually get it back by starting again with a new egg, as you would for a mayonnaise, and just adding the curdled mixture *very* slowly. However, if it has gone beyond recall and you have neither the time nor the enthusiasm to start again, throw all caution to the winds! Boil the sauce so as to thoroughly scramble the eggs, pour off the butter (to be used for something else) and serve the curdled egg as an interesting side dish instead of a sauce. Your guests will probably never even guess – unless they too have bought this book!

You may, wisely, prefer to employ preventative techniques. Either a teaspoonful of cornflour beaten into the egg yolks before you start, or a tablespoonful of béchamel sauce beaten into the cooked Hollandaise as soon as it is ready, will keep the sauce in one piece, although it does alter the texture. Alternatively, make the sauce in the blender, which is *almost* foolproof as long as you add the melted butter very slowly. The texture is noticeably different from handmade Hollandaise, but do you care as long as it is in one piece?

Mayonnaise

In the sauce family, mayonnaise is Hollandaise's more phlegmatic cousin – 'can

be difficult if she's in a bad mood but not totally unreliable'. The trouble maker is, of course, the egg yolk, which puts an arbitrary limit on the amount of foreign material the sauce will take on board. Mayonnaise is also affected by the weather and should be avoided on a humid or thundery day. Having said that, provided all the ingredients are at room temperature and patience is exercised, success should attend your efforts.

Mixing

As with Hollandaise, mayonnaise is much easier to make in an electric mixer, liquidizer or food processor than by hand, but the consistency is different. If it is to be hand-made, the yolk of the egg alone is needed; if it is to be 'electrified', then the whole egg. If making by hand, beat the yolk for a couple of min-

utes with 1–2 teaspoons of lemon juice or vinegar to stabilize it, before you start adding the oil, and then add it in drips only – 1 yolk will absorb approximately ¼ pint/150 ml/1⅔ cups of oil. 'Electrified' mayonnaise will absorb almost twice as much but, although the oil can be added somewhat faster, the principle is exactly the same – as are the rescue methods if it decides to curdle on you.

Curdling

If this happens, take out the curdled mixture, clean out the bowl and start again with a new egg or yolk to which you very gradually add the curdled mayonnaise. You can also beat a tablespoon of made mustard and use that as the base for your new mayonnaise. If either of these methods fail, then you should change your oil. Most vegetable and salad oils will make acceptable

mayonnaise (the most flavourful are olive, nut or sunflower oil). Occasionally, though, you meet an oil to which the egg takes a violent dislike and nothing you can do will persuade it to absorb it.

Adjusting flavour

Flavourless mayonnaise is easily remedied – merely add a *little* more seasoning, lemon juice or vinegar until you have an acceptable flavour. Overseasoned mayonnaise is more difficult. If it is only slightly overdone, add more oil, if it will take it, or cream or yoghurt. These will change the texture and flavour somewhat, but will help kill the salt, pepper or vinegar. If it is badly overseasoned, you should remove half and keep if for another day and merely tone down what is left – you will otherwise end up with an enormous amount of mayonnaise and have no cream left for the dessert.

Cheating

If you cannot cope with making your own, there are several excellent brands of manufactured mayonnaises, but be sure that it is mayonnaise, not 'salad cream', 'salad dressing' or any other euphemism for emulsified vinegar and sugar. To transform it into all your own, add some cream, yoghurt, horseradish, good mustard, curry paste, chopped watercress or herbs, tabasco, finely chopped peppers, garlic, or indeed anything you have around that will complement the meal.

Vinaigrette dressings

These are merely mayonnaise without the egg and are therefore quite safe in texture, although care should be taken not to over- or under-flavour them. A little too much vinegar or lemon juice is very much more difficult to counterbalance than a little too much oil. The normal proportions are 1 tablespoon of vinegar to 3 of oil. Again, remove half of

the dressing for another day and merely rectify the overseasoning of the remaining half. Almost any additive is good in an oil and vinegar dressing – feel free to experiment, but only do so in small quantities so that if it doesn't work, it is not too late to counteract it.

Tomato sauce

Home-made tomato sauce can so easily be the elixir of the gods that it is tragic how often it turns up as a pink, watery plosh. The secret is long and gentle cooking to concentrate the flavour of the tomatoes, be they fresh or tinned. If you do not have the time for this, then drain off the liquid and reinforce the flavour with some tomato paste – *not* tomato ketchup.

Bread sauce

Bread sauce too can go from the supreme to the really horrible. Like tomato sauce, it depends on long, slow cooking to mature the flavours of the onion, cloves, bread and milk. If this cannot be managed, a passable bread sauce can be achieved by amalgamating a good packet of onion sauce with a half-cooked bread sauce.

Packet sauces

There are many excellent packet and tinned sauces that can be pressed into service in time of need. It usually pays to dilute them less than instructed and to do so with stock, vegetable water or a mixture of wine and water. If you are using a packet, 'home-made' touches such as chopped parsley or chives, finely sliced mushrooms or, if you are feeling extravagant, truffles, good seasoning and a splash of sherry or wine will form a very effective disguise.

Eggs

Such innocent little things, eggs, yet what culinary horrors they are responsible for. They bedevil sauces and haunt meringues, make leathery omelettes and lumpy scrambled egg, and as for the traumas they cause as soufflés! But they can be the quickest and most useful of foods so it is worth trying to make a truce with them if you can.

Eggs crop up in almost every form of cooking – which makes life very difficult for those unfortunates who cannot eat them – but on their own they are normally restricted to boiled, fried or baked. Boiling (to include poaching) really is simple and can only be ruined by being over- or under-done. Frying involves not only fried eggs, which come sunny-side-up (or down), but scrambled eggs and omelettes, which are 'beaten up' first and fried rather more gently. Baking covers the thorny territory of soufflés, those little pots of eggs that should be served soft or '*moux*' and are so often bullet-like, and egg custard flans or quiches.

Boiling

Boiled eggs

It sounds easy to say that boiled eggs can only be spoiled by over- or undercooking but more tempers have been soured and marriages broken by wrongly cooked breakfast eggs than any other form of food! An overcooked soft-boiled egg is beyond recall. Some amelioration may be achieved by adding butter to it but the only real answer is to start again. An undercooked boiled egg can, with care, be brought to perfection. Tie it, broken side up, in a piece of muslin,

tea cloth or anything that is clean and to hand, and suspend it in the boiling water. You can just hold it, but if it is badly undercooked, tie the ends of the cloth round a wooden spoon laid across the top of the pan.

A hard-boiled egg, if overcooked, will get a grey line round the outside of the yolk. This will not affect the flavour but it doesn't look too good. If this happens, all you can do is chop the egg (when it effectively vanishes), or slice it and then cover it with a mayonnaise sauce.

Poached eggs

Poached eggs are a little more hazardous, as the white is no longer kept in check by the shell. The easy way out is to use an egg poacher, which restrains the white within a mould. However, if you want to live dangerously, add a little vinegar to the simmering water – the acid will help to stabilize the egg white. Stir the water around with the handle of a wooden spoon or some such implement until you create a deep vortex into which you drop your egg. You need to do this as fast as possible so that the water continues to whirl round the egg, keeping it in a neat shape in the middle. It helps if you break the egg into a cup or saucer so that you can tip it straight in with one hand while you are whirling with the other. The time it takes to cook will depend on the size of the egg, but with the water simmering gently it will normally be between 3 and 4½ minutes – slightly less than a boiled egg, as the heat does not have to penetrate the shell. To know whether it is cooked, hold it in a slotted spoon and shake it gently – if the white is firm then the yolk is done. If you allow the water to boil, it will fritter the white and make for an untidy egg.

To remove the egg you need a slotted spoon, not a fish slice – off which it would take great delight in slipping . . . Make sure that as much water as possible drains off, as there is nothing nastier than a poached egg on a sodden slice of toast.

If you overcook a poached egg, there is nothing you can do about it; if you undercook it, slip it back into the spoon and just hold it in the water for another 30 seconds or so.

Incidentally, never be tempted to put salt rather than vinegar into the water; far from stabilizing the white, the salt will break it down so that it fritters and breaks away from the yolk.

Frying

Fried eggs

Fried eggs can be overcooked, cooked in dirty fat, which gives them a nasty flavour and spots them all over with the remains of last night's supper, or get their yolks broken.

Oil, butter, bacon fat or dripping are all good egg fryers but in each case they should be clean or new. Fried eggs should be cooked with reasonable expedition but, if the fat is too hot, they will burn and frizzle on the bottom before the yolk and top half of the white are set. To avoid this, make sure there is plenty of fat or oil in the pan and spoon it over the eggs as they cook so that the top gets cooked by the hot fat. The yolk should be cooked when the white is set – if you wait till the yolk looks cooked, it will be overdone.

You do need a decent fish slice to get a fried egg out in one piece. Just ease it gently under the egg and then lift. If you do break the yolk, either just serve it and ignore the flowing yellow river or whip it quickly over onto the other side, cook it briefly to set the yolk and serve it as an American fried egg – 'over easy' is the correct terminology.

Scrambled eggs

Scrambled eggs and omelettes are similar in that both have their eggs whisked and lightly diluted – one with milk or cream, the other with water.

Scrambled eggs should be cooked very slowly in a thick-bottomed pan over a very low heat. The eggs should never sizzle and should set in large globules, which can be gently turned over to allow the rest to cook.

Scrambled eggs need constant attention to maintain their texture, stirring or folding gently whenever the bit nearest the heat is cooked. As with fried eggs, if they start to look well cooked they are overdone. You should remove the pan when there is still some liquid egg surrounding the cooked – by the time the scrambled eggs get to the toast or the table they will be sufficiently done. Serve on warm, not hot, plates; if the plate is too hot the scrambled eggs will frizzle when they touch it and you will get frilly overcooked edges.

Scrambled eggs should never be dried up or tough. However, should they, by some mischance, manage to get that way . . . If not too bad, you can pour a little cream over as disguise and grind some black pepper on top. If they are beyond recall, give up the idea of scrambled eggs. Turn them onto some toast or a heatproof dish, sprinkle with some cheese, put under the grill and pretend you are serving up a Welsh Rarebit. Or, cook the eggs till they are solid, chop them finely and use as a garnish for stew, soups, salads or even a risotto. Or cook till hard, cool them, mix with some mayonnaise and make into a mousse or sandwich filling.

Omelettes

An omelette, by contrast, is cooked very quickly over a very high heat in very hot butter. However, no more than scrambled egg should it ever be hard or leathery. The secret of keeping it moist is speed – cook it very quickly using a spatula or fork to pull the cooked mixture in from the sides so that the uncooked mixture can come in direct contact with the sizzling pan.

Never try to make an omelette with more than 6 eggs. To achieve a successful omelette approximately a third of the total mixture should be in contact with the surface of the pan. More than 6 eggs make so much bulk that you would need a monster pan to achieve the right relationship. All that will happen is that the eggs will cook too slowly, thus setting all through like scrambled egg. To lighten an omelette, add a generous tablespoon of cold water for every 2 eggs and beat well.

As with scrambled egg, there should always be some liquid egg left when you finish cooking, especially if you are adding filling. The time it takes to add the filling and the residual heat in the pan will be quite enough to finish off the cooking process. Again, always serve an omelette on a warm, not hot, plate.

If, despite your best endeavours, the omelette does go hard and leathery, you could cover it with a sauce – tomato or cheese, for example. Once the omelette is cooked, it will keep, off the heat, quite happily while you make, defrost or de-tin the sauce – although you may have problems with your guests who are sitting waiting for their omelette! Alternatively, turn the omelette, like the scrambled eggs, into Welsh Rarebit or abandon for future use as a garnish and start again.

Apart from actual texture, the most common hazard is the omelette's occasional and passionate refusal to part company with the pan. Normally this happens when the pan has been used for cooking something like bacon, which leaves a heavy salty residue, but even the most perfect omelette pans can turn nasty. To guard against such an event, try to keep one pan only for cooking omelettes and never use any form of soap when you clean it. A good wipe with paper towel should be sufficient to clean a pan after a well-cooked omelette.

If the pan needs more, rub really well with coarse salt and then polish with oil and paper towel. If you must use water, never use soap, and rub well with oil as soon as the pan is dry. A new pan should be filled with ½ inch/1.25 cm of oil and some coarse salt, be left to soak for 12 hours and then heated till the oil smokes. The oil should then be poured out and the pan wiped dry with paper towel. It will also help if you use clarified or unsalted butter, as both the salt and the water in ordinary butter encourage sticking.

However, if the world turns against you and the omelette sticks, take the pan off the heat and use a fish slice to prise the omelette off the bottom as tidily as you can, then turn it onto the plate. It will not have a perfectly browned outside, but, hopefully, it will remain reasonably in one piece and will taste fine. If you have them, sprinkle some chopped parsley, herbs or even black pepper over the top as disguise.

Baking

Baked eggs

Baked eggs are the simplest thing in the world – provided they do not overcook themselves. Your only hope is to stick rigidly to the recipe, giving them exactly the time required. Do *not* wait until the eggs look well set, as they will by then have gone too far. Do not forget that the eggs continue to cook in their dishes after you have taken them out of the oven. If you are at all nervous about overcooking, have some sauce ready that can be spooned over the eggs so that they do not taste dried up, even if the yolk is a little too hard. If you go completely wrong and they are like bullets, it is better to scoop each one out of its ramekin dish, put them all in one serving dish, spoon over a sauce and garnish well – with yesterday's chopped up, overcooked omelette maybe? They will then look as though you intended them that way, which they never will if they are in individual pots!

Quiches

Quiches are such popular and useful things that it is a shame that they are so often uneatable. The worst offender is often the pastry, which, through no fault of the egg, is grey, leaden and soggy. Always bake a quiche case blind (empty) and make sure it is cooked right through. Preferably both bake it blind and paint it with egg white, which you dry off in the oven in an attempt to persuade it to remain crisp.

When it comes to making the filling, whisk the eggs and milk together with a balloon whisk before adding the filling, as this helps to lighten the mixture. Do not overload the custard with filling. One of the beauties of a well-made quiche is the light egg custard; if it is too heavily laden, you will not be able to taste the custard and the eggs will be quite unable to lift such a burden of filling. However, that does not mean that it should not be well flavoured. Both eggs and milk are bland, so unless you are using a very powerful filling, such as anchovies, you will need to season the mixture generously.

As with most egg dishes, the important thing is not to cook the quiche too fast. If you allow it to boil, the egg and liquid will curdle and separate. Instead of a light and airy custard you will get globules of overcooked egg and filling floating in a watery lake held together by soggy pastry. If this happens, the only person it should be offered to is the cat – who will probably refuse it! Forty-

five minutes to 1 hour in a moderately slow oven (300°F/150°C/Gas Mark 2) should be about right for most quiches.

Soufflés

Of all egg dishes, soufflés must be the most feared and, when they work, the most effective. Yet they are not difficult, as long as one understands the principles on which they are based. Nonetheless, if you are a beginner (or a duffer) at soufflé making, try it out on the family first, or have an alternative dish ready in case of emergencies.

In a soufflé one uses the air-trapping properties of whisked egg white combined with the heat of the oven to increase the mixture to almost double its bulk. The heat of the oven causes the air held in the egg white to expand, thereby raising the whole edifice. Meanwhile, the setting powers of the egg yolks ensure that the mixture, expanded in the early stages of cooking, retains its new bulk. Provided the amount of air that is trapped in the mixture is in proportion to the bulk it is required to lift, and provided that sufficient heat is applied to it, the soufflé cannot fail to rise and set. Whether it rises more or less, retains its elevation, or falls back somewhat when it comes out of the oven, is brown on top or crusty round the sides, are all refinements on the basic principle.

The normal proportions for a soufflé are 2 oz/50 g butter to 1½ oz/40 g flour to ½ pint/300 ml/1¼ cups of liquid for the white sauce that forms the base of the soufflé. To that you will need to add 4 egg yolks, 3–6 oz/75–175 g of flavouring, depending on what it is, and 5 egg whites – always 1 more white than yolk. This will be enough for 4–6 people, depending on whether it is to be served as a starter, main course or dessert. These proportions can be increased or decreased according to the number of people to be fed and the flavouring substance you are using. If it is rather heavy (a fish such as crab, for example, as opposed to a strong cheese; chocolate as opposed to a liqueur), you may need an extra white to give more lifting power.

Once the basic sauce is made, the flavouring needs to be added in ample quantity. It must be remembered that a large bulk of egg whites and air (both totally flavourless) is going to be added to the mixture, so it should really taste quite powerful at the sauce stage. If you are using a vegetable flavouring that has been puréed, make sure that all the water has been evaporated out of it. Egg white can cope with lifting a certain amount of bulk, but water is extremely heavy, and watery vegetables will weigh down a soufflé. This is particularly important with vegetables, such as courgettes (zucchini), that are by nature very wet. Once the flavouring and seasoning is in and well amalgamated, remove the sauce from the heat before adding the egg yolk, otherwise the yolk will cook before it gets into the oven.

Whisking the egg whites is almost the most important part of the whole operation. They must be whisked in an absolutely clean, dry bowl and no speck of yolk must be allowed to appear or they will refuse to whip at all. Incidentally, if a speck of egg yolk does intrude, it is much easier to remove with a piece of shell than with a spoon. A pinch of salt, cream of tartar, or the use of a copper bowl will help the whipping process. Use a hand whisk or a balloon whisk rather than an electric one, as it is easier to involve all the egg white in the whipping process all the time – an electric beater will tend only to whisk the bit in the middle of the bowl. Do not whisk the whites too stiff; they should hold their shapes in soft peaks. If you whisk them till they are totally stiff (as for meringues), they will become dry and brittle and will be impossible to fold evenly into the sauce mixture. When they are

ready, gently stir about a third of the egg whites into the sauce – this will lighten the sauce and make it easier to fold in the rest. Fold in what remains and make sure that they are as well amalgamated as possible with the sauce. Do not fold more than necessary, as you are only breaking the bubbles in the egg whites and letting your precious air escape.

It is best to use a soufflé dish that will be about two-thirds or three-quarters filled by your mixture. This means that the mixture should rise up well above the edge of the dish without rising so far above it that it risks falling over. If you grease the inside of the dish, it will allow the soufflé to slide more easily up it – but you will not get the crunchy outside edge that many soufflé lovers fight over. There is no particular virtue in heating the dish beforehand – this merely tends to cook the outside faster, forming a crust that may inhibit rising.

One of the major hazards of soufflé making is not the soufflé but the unpunctuality of guests, as you cannot ask a soufflé to wait more than 5 minutes to be eaten. However you can quite successfully keep a soufflé that is ready for the oven in the fridge for up to 4 hours, whipping it into the oven as soon as the malingerers appear. If you do this, you must allow an extra 10 minutes cooking time. Alternatively, you can make it the day before and freeze it; it will take rather longer to cook (between 20 and 30 minutes, depending on the size of the soufflé), but it does save a last minute panic. In both cases, the soufflé will lose a little in fluffiness, but not enough to

bother any but the most fastidious cook.

Once you come to actually cooking the thing, you must be sure that your oven is up to temperature before the soufflé goes in – you do not want the egg yolks to cook and set the mixture before the air in the whites has expanded enough to raise it. A moderately hot oven is recommended by most cooks: 350–375°F/180–190°C/Gas Mark 4–5. If the oven is too cool, the air expansion will not be sufficient to raise the soufflé as much as you might hope. It will be perfectly acceptable but more like a steamed pudding than a soufflé. If the oven is too hot, the air will expand too quickly for the egg yolk to keep up, so that as soon as it comes out of the oven and the ambient temperature drops, the air in the soufflé will contract. Since the egg yolk will not have had time to solidify properly, it will be unable to hold it up. The result will be that the soufflé will fall rather quickly, although not so quickly that you will not be able to rush it to the table to a chorus of admiring oohs and aahs and plunge the spoon in before it collapses! If the oven is too hot, it may also form a crust on the outside, which will prevent the inside cooking properly.

However, if the temperature is right, the rising of the egg white and the cooking of the yolk should happen simultaneously, thereby getting it to rise and stay risen. To achieve this successfully, the heat should come from the bottom of the oven. It helps to put a metal sheet under the soufflé dish, which concentrates the heat under the dish. It goes without saying that one should not continually open the oven in which the soufflé is cooking, as this alters the oven temperature and prevents the even cooking that is so important. Twenty-five to 30 minutes should be enough for the average soufflé if you want the centre slightly runny; if you want it cooked right through, 30–35 minutes. If necessary, you can test it with something very fine like a thin knitting needle, exactly as you would test a cake.

Of course there does remain a slight risk of failure . . .

Underestimating the degree to which a soufflé may rise and putting it too high in the oven has caused many a soufflé to rush upwards, collide with the top of the oven and remain firmly glued to it! All you can do is to scrape the beautifully browned upper layer off and serve the soufflé from a side table so that no one can see!

More likely will be a failure to rise as much as it should have done – this will mean that it has the texture of a

to the filling and whip it under the grill so that it ends up brown and crunchy on top, which will contrast nicely with the soggy middle. If it is a sweet soufflé, treat it the same way but sprinkle it with sugar and caramelize it under the grill, or, if the filling is suitable, pour a jam sauce over it as though it were a sweet omelette.

Timbales

The safer way altogether to make soufflés is to steam them, but this achieves a quite different, though very pleasant, texture. They become *timbales*, or moulds, and can be eaten hot or cold. The principles for making them are the same as for soufflés and the proportions are similar. The difference lies in the fact that they are baked in a *bain-marie* or steamed on the top of the cooker and they are cooked slightly more slowly. When they are turned out, they are usually coated with a light sauce.

steamed pudding rather than a soufflé. If this happens, either serve it as a '*pouding soufflé*', or have a sauce prepared for such a moment and serve it with its accompanying sauce, so it will look as though you intended it that way all along.

If it really has failed to rise at all, the best bet is to treat it like an overcooked omelette. Spoon it out of the dish onto a platter, maybe on to some toast, sprinkle it with cheese or something suitable

Opposite: *Who said that mayonnaise is easy to make? To reconstitute your curdled bowlful, see page 29.*

If your cheese soufflé sinks miserably – spoon it into a new dish, sprinkle it heavily with cheese, and grill.

Opposite: *Has your delicious loganberry mousse unmoulded itself in a battered heap? Push the pieces back together and disguise with cream, mimosa balls, kiwi fruit and cherries.*

Below: *What* do *you do with that solid mass of white stodge? Mix the rice thoroughly with a tin of chopped tomatoes and olives, breadcrumbs and seasoning. Form it into balls and bake for 10 minutes. You won't recognize it!*

Pâtés, Mousses and Jellies

Pâtés and terrines

Pâtés and terrines are usually solid and cooked, although there are some pâtés (smoked fish, for example) that are merely amalgamated. These uncooked pâtés are extremely easy to make and almost indestructible as long as you taste them frequently to make sure that you get the proportion of butter to fish and the seasoning right.

A pâté or terrine can range from a lovingly prepared and extremely complex French masterpiece – a veritable *chef d'oeuvre* – to the twin brother to a meat loaf. Flavour is cooked into the pâté, so it is difficult to alter it at the last moment except by serving it with a 'toning down' or 'beefing up' sauce. However, most pâtés are made with well-flavoured meats, so tastelessness is not usually a problem. They do need a fair proportion of fat but, since most pâtés involve bacon somewhere in their makeup, this is built in. Cooking in a *bain-marie* also helps to keep them

moist. If, nonetheless, your pâté turns out to be rather dry, the best answer once again is to serve it with a sauce, a chutney or a fruit preserve.

Falling apart

The most common problem with cooked pâtés is their refusal to stay in one piece when you come to cut them. This normally means that the pâté was not sufficiently well weighted when it came out of the oven. Weighting with about 2 lb/ 1 kg for a normal size pâté is essential if it is to pack down into a solid mass. If you discover in time that your beautiful pâté is in danger of disintegrating, you can add some gelled meat stock or stiffened consommé. If you have not got time for this, turn it into a bowl and serve it as a soft pâté. You may want to put it through a food processor to 'smooth it up a bit' if it is to be served from a bowl. If it is only marginally soft, cut it with a hot knife, which will penetrate more easily.

Freezing

Pâtés with a high proportion of jelly or liquid in them do not freeze well. The jelly tends to liquify and the texture breaks down in the course of freezing. When the pâtés defrost, they will do so in a lake of juice. All you can do is to

Opposite: *Did the pastry stick to the board, roll itself out to the wrong shape and maliciously tear itself as it climbed over the steak and kidney pie? Use the remains to patch with leaves, bobbles, or whatever, and paint liberally with beaten egg to make a golden pastry tableau.*

mop up the juice and decorate them with lots of fresh watercress or parsley to disguise their rather soggy texture. The flavour will be slightly impaired, but not unacceptably. Solid pâtés, such as the smoked fish and butter pâtés, freeze excellently.

Mousses and cold soufflés

Mousses and cold soufflés have two chronic defects: an unwillingness to gel correctly and a tendency to be tasteless.

What changes a mousse into a cold soufflé is the whisked egg white that is added to the latter to give it a fluffier texture. A soufflé is also normally made in a dish with a collar of greaseproof paper around it so it can stand proud of the dish when set. A mousse is merely puréed avocado, chicken, fruit or chocolate, for example, mixed with a sauce, whipped cream and gelatine.

Flavour

Because of the blandness of so many of the ingredients, and because their taste will be deadened further by chilling, it is important to flavour and season them well. If you fail to do so, you can melt the whole thing down again (very gently over a bowl of hot water), add more flavouring and reset. This is even possible with a soufflé, although the result will be mousse-like in texture, as the egg whites will inevitably lose their texture in the melting. However, a simpler answer is to serve a well-flavoured sauce as an accompaniment/disguise.

Of course, it is always possible to overdo your quest for flavour. If you do, some extra cream will usually correct the fault.

Setting

The gelling process is a little more difficult to get right. The quantity of gelatine required to set 1 pint/600 ml/2½ cups of liquid is normally ½ oz/15 g gelatine. When dealing with a mousse or soufflé mixture, you start with a much stiffer 'liquid' so that half this amount should be sufficient. On the other hand, an acid fruit, such as pineapple or lemon, may require more. The recipe will usually give the correct amount for that combination of food.

When dealing with a mousse, you should not have any problems, as all the ingredients are amalgamated and then chilled. However, take care that the melted gelatine and the purée it is to thicken are approximately the same temperature when you amalgamate them. If hot liquid gelatine is mixed into a cold base, it will gel immediately and you will get a solid rope of gelatine run-

ning through your mixture. If this happens, melt the whole thing over some boiling water until the gelatine softens again – this will not do much for your whipped cream but it is better than 'ropy' mousse!

Separating

Sweet soufflés and mousses, because they normally contain a higher proportion of liquid than their savoury siblings, sometimes separate leaving a gooey or liquid layer in the bottom. You can unmould them, remix, add more whisked egg white or cream and rechill.

However, since some of the most *recherché* dishes are designed in layers it would be a lot easier to look your guests straight in the eye and say you have just found this *wonderful* recipe for chocolate mousse that has a delicious layer of goo in the bottom! Alternatively, unmould the whole thing and treat the runny layer as a sauce that has been carefully poured over the top.

Unmoulding

If you decide to unmould your mousse, dip the dish fairly briefly into boiling water to loosen the filling. You can always dip it again but too long a submersion melts the outside layer of the mousse and causes it to run all over the dish when it comes out. If this happens, clean up the dish and decorate heavily – parsley, watercress, slices of fruit, chopped jelly, etc. – or, if you have time, cover the whole thing with sweet or savoury jelly.

On the other hand, it may come out in several pieces. You will usually be able to replace them roughly where they ought to go. After that it is up to the decoration. If you have time it is worth using jelly to decorate, as you will be able to completely disguise the cracks and fissures – see page 49.

If, however, you want to guard against the possibility of disintegration, make the mousse in a loose-bottomed cake tin lined with greaseproof paper or cling film to prevent it running out of the cracks. You will be able to lift the mousse up through the ring part of the mould till it meets the plate it is to go on and then up-end it so that it does not fall with a sickening splat onto the plate, shattering itself as it does so. You then only need to carefully peel off the cling film or greaseproof paper.

If you want to use a fancy mould, line the mould with cling film. You may get a slight 'creasing' effect on the outside of the jelly or mousse but at least you can guarantee that it will come out!

Mixing in egg whites

With a soufflé, you need to add the whisked egg whites right at the end of the process. If the base is not reasonably well set, the egg whites will not be able to support it; if it is too set, you will not be able to amalgamate it properly and you will have lumps of already set mousse mixed with globules of egg white. If this happens, you will just have to melt down the base again and then re-gel it to the right degree of stiffness. It needs to be the texture of lightly whipped cream and the only way to achieve this is to keep an eagle eye on it in the fridge until it makes the grade.

Failure to set

If, perchance, either mixture fails to gel altogether, if you have time, melt down the half set mousse over hot water, then melt more gelatine (not more than half the total quantity required for the whole recipe) in a little hot water. Cool this, mix it well into the mousse and reset. If you do not have time, spoon it into tall glasses and call it 'a cream'.

Whisking yolks over hot water

Some cold soufflés require that the egg yolks and sugar be whisked over hot water till they thicken. It is possible to overcook and curdle or scramble the egg mixture. If you do, take it immediately off the heat and plunge the bowl into cold water. Provided you catch it early enough, the slight deterioration in texture will be lost in the soufflé mixture. If, on the other hand, it refuses to thicken, it means that your water is not hot enough to cook the egg yolk and thereby thicken the mixture.

Jellies

The saviour of many a boring or disintegrated mousse or soufflé is a jelly decoration – either a clear jelly or a stiffened mayonnaise, *chaudfroid* or sweetened cream. This can, of course, go wrong itself but, if it works, it will cover a multitude of sins.

Boiling gelatine

One is always warned not to boil gelatine. Prolonged boiling will eventually break it down, and also as it boils some of the mixture will dry on the side of your container so that you lose some of your gel. However, modern gelatine is quite tolerant and you need not abandon it immediately if it has crept up to a boil when it was only meant to be melting.

Aspic

The best aspic is undoubtedly homemade – not really too much of a sweat if you have the time. However, excellent substitutes can be made with commercial aspic – especially if you add a little sherry to the water you melt it in – or tins of consommé, which also benefit from a splash of sherry. Be careful which brand you use though, as some have very 'canned' flavours. Before using a tinned consommé, check how firmly it gels, most of them set quite soft and may need the addition of a little gelatine.

Chaudfroid

An opaque or *chaudfroid* glaze can be made from a good éspagnole, béchamel or velouté sauce thickened with gelatine. Substitute, but equally effective, *chaudfroid* can be based on mayonnaise or double cream boiled with a little appropriate stock, some herbs and seasoning. You will need approximately ¼ oz/10 g gelatine for 1 pint/600 ml/ 2½ cups of the sauce. A brown *chaudfroid* is traditionally used to decorate tongues and boars' heads; a white is used for chicken, turkey or fish.

Gelatine

There is no virtue at all in making one's own gelatine! Commercial gelatines mixed with strained fruit juices, sweet wines or mixtures of juices and liqueurs make excellent clear jellies. If an opaque jelly is needed, double cream, lightly sweetened (melt the sugar with the gelatine) will work very well.

Decorating with jelly

The secret of decorating with clear or opaque jelly is to get the mixture to the syrupy consistency where it is still just pourable but will cling to what you are decorating and set quickly. Always make more jelly than you need and chill it on a flat plate or baking tray. It can then be cut up into little squares and used to cover all imperfections! Use a teaspoon to spoon the jelly over the 'subject' – a tablespoon can get out of hand.

Once the first layer has set, you can use herbs, black olives, fruit, crystallized flowers or anything else that comes to hand to decorate and make a pretty pattern. Dip whatever it is in the liquid jelly and place it in position – a pair of tweezers is quite helpful – it prevents you from messing up the jelly with your fingers. Obviously, if you are using a white *chaudfroid*, you merely place the

naked decorations on the white base. If you are feeling very ambitious, you can then paint the whole thing with a clear jelly.

This sort of decoration is invaluable if the mousse has failed to unmould itself in one piece. Merely place your decoration strategically and cover with

another layer of jelly. If it runs down the side, it doesn't matter as you can use the chopped squares to cover any unsightly pools. Even if you totally mess up the decoration you can scrape the whole lot off, carefully, melt it down and start again! However, do ensure that each layer is well set before you embark on the next, otherwise you will find yourself with a floating lake of decorations.

When decorating a mousse or, indeed, a galantine or pâté, it is best to just place it in the fridge to gel between each layer. If you are being ambitious and want to line a mould with gelatine before putting in the mousse, you will find it easiest to use a bowl of ice in which you can move the mould as you coat its sides with aspic.

Decorated jellies

Of course, you can make a decorated jelly by merely suspending eggs, ham, spinach, fruits, sweets or whatever you want in jelly. If you do this, make sure that the jelly is very well flavoured, as it has nothing to help it along. Also, if you are using something solid like ham, cut it up fairly small, otherwise the jelly will fall apart completely when you try to serve it.

Freezing

Gelatine does not mind being frozen as long as it is incorporated in a relatively firm liaison such as a mousse, but it will not survive if you attempt to freeze it alone. When it defrosts, it will liquify and you will have to start again. Even when incorporated in a mousse, it may lose some of its power but probably not enough to materially affect the consistency. Should it do so, you would have no option but to reset with new gelatine.

Pastry

Pastry making is a business that unnerves even experienced cooks. But, as long as you abide by a few basic rules, the simpler pastries should present no real problems. Of course, once you embark on the puff and flaky pastries it is a different matter . . . There are, however, certain fundamental principles that apply to all types of pastry.

Proportions

The proportion of fat to flour to water must be right no matter what type of pastry you're making. The sort of fat used is a matter of personal preference. I normally use a combination of butter and lard for shortcrust (white or wholemeal) and flaky, but margarine is perfectly acceptable and preferred by some. In hot weather, fats get very soft and tempt the cook to add less water. But too little water makes the pastry dry and crumbly; too much makes it leaden. If in doubt, chill the mixture before adding the water – this will return the fat and flour mixture to its normal consistency. Chilling pastry can never do it any harm and often improves it.

Handling

Handle (which includes rubbing, kneading and rolling) the pastry as little as possible. In cooking, the ingredients in underkneaded or badly mixed pastry will amalgamate reasonably well but too much kneading, handling or rolling just makes it tough.

Cooking

Undercooked pastry will always be soggy and nasty. Put it back in the oven even at the risk of overcooking the contents. Overcooked pastry is better, as it is at least crisp – although blackened crust is irretrievable! If you do burn it beyond repair, scrape off the crust and cover the pie, if savoury, with plain breadcrumbs, then brown them *lightly* under the grill. If the pie is sweet, mix the crumbs with a little brown sugar and then sprinkle on top and brown under the grill.

Pie lids will get cooked on the outside but remain soggy inside unless you make small slashes in the lid to allow the steam from their cooking contents to escape. Ideally, this should be done after the pie has been in the oven long enough for the crust to harden into shape.

Patching

No matter how perfect your pastry, it may tear as it is rolled out. It helps to lift it over a rolling pin rather than with your hands. If you are lining a flan case, use little bits of pastry to patch the cracks or tears. Moisten the base before applying the patch and press it down. If it is a pie lid, use the pastry trimmings to make some decoration – a leaf is the simplest and often the most effective, although little pastry balls are even easier and will cover a multitude of sins. Be inventive with the trimmings: a pastry eel weaving its way across the lid of a fish pie can not only cover the crack but look very impressive.

Shrinkage

Your flan case or pie top may shrink in the cooking, especially if the pastry was too wet, or if you did not leave enough overlap at the edge of the flan dish or stick the edges of the pastry well down. If you are making a case for a deep-dish pie, you will need to leave the pastry hanging well over the edge to stop it shrinking down the sides of the dish into a roll at the bottom. This can happen even with a shallow flan case, although it should not, as long as you have not stretched the pastry over the edge instead of pushing it well into the corners. If either does shrink and you can catch it before it is cooked, you can usually ease the pastry back up the side again but it will be difficult to secure. It might be better to cut out the shrunken roll and replace it with new pastry sides that are firmly stuck to the base and hang over the edge of the dish.

It is possible to go on patching till quite late in the cooking process. If you discover halfway through its cooking that the lid of the pie has also shrunk, you can take it out, patch it, glaze the patch and return it to the oven. The patch will cook more quickly than the rest because there is less of it.

If you do not discover till too late, you can stick parsley all round in the gap, but it is probably better just to serve it straight onto the plates from a side table. Once you have cut into the pie, no one will be able to see what it looked like at the beginning.

Bubbling

If you do not weight your flan case with foil and some rice or beans when you bake it blind (empty), you may get air bubbles in the base. If you catch them before the case is cooked, pierce them to allow the air to escape, then weight the case. If it is already cooked, it will usually only have raised the top layer of paste, so you can break it and leave the broken bits lying in the bottom. If you are through to the dish, provided the case is to be cooked again (a quiche case, for example), you can still patch it with new pastry. If it is not to be recooked, you may be able to seal a small hole with egg white. Alternatively, make the filling fairly solid!

Insufficient pastry

If you have not made enough pastry for a flan, abandon the sides and only cover the bottom of the dish to make a sort of pastry plate bottom. Line the sides with foil to stop the contents sticking to the sides and running under the base. You should be able to peel off the foil carefully when the dish is cooked.

If it is a pie, cut the available pastry into long strips and make a lattice-work top.

Insufficient filling

If you do not put enough filling into your pie, the lid will sink. If you are at all concerned, support the middle with a pie funnel or an egg cup, upside down. Once the pie is cooked, there is not a lot you can do about a sunken lid – except serve it in the kitchen far from prying eyes.

Shortcrust pastry

The most usual proportions are half fat to flour and 3–4 tablespoons of water to 8 oz/225 g/2 cups of flour. However, the exact amount of water you need to achieve a pliable dough does vary and getting it exactly right is a matter of experience.

In hot weather, shortcrust pastry is particularly likely to fool you into thinking you should reduce the quantity of liquid. If you are dubious, chill the mixture before adding the water. If you

do find yourself with totally dry and crumbling paste, do not try to roll it out at all. Press it out into scone shapes with your hand and use these to cover the pie or the base of the flan case. If a pie, glaze well and say it is a regional/traditional/new and revolutionary way of making pie crust.

Hot water crust

Provided you follow the recipe (making sure the water is boiling before you add it to the flour), the only problem likely to arise is at the moulding stage. If you try to mould it when it is too hot, it will not keep its shape and will slither down the side of the mould. If it is too cold, it will solidify and crumble and you will be able to do nothing with it at all. If this happens and you have a microwave, cover the pastry and put it in the oven for about 30 seconds – enough to warm it up without starting the cooking process. If you do not have a microwave, put the bowl over some hot water – but be careful not to have the water too hot – and turn the lump of paste frequently, otherwise it will melt on one side and remain rock solid on the other.

Choux pastry

Eggs

Follow the proportions for the recipe but be careful not to add all the eggs at one time. Depending on the size of the eggs and the consistency of the flour, the stated number of eggs may make the whole mixture too runny. It should be a firm 'piping' consistency and thick enough to hold its shape easily when you place a spoonful on a tray. If the mixture reaches this stage before you have added all the eggs, leave one out. If it is too late and it is already too runny, you will have to make another small amount of the flour, butter and water mixture – probably no more than a quarter of the total amount in the recipe, although that depends on how runny your mixture is. Make this exactly as normal and then beat it into the runny mixture. Beat the whole thing well so that the two amalgamate.

Beating

Do not beat too much in the early stages before adding the eggs, otherwise the profiteroles will become rather spongy.

If this happens, do not worry about it – tell your guests that it is a recipe you have discovered that originates from the south of France.

Shaping

Some people find it easier to pipe profiteroles with a bag, but this will only work if the paste is still warm – unless you have Superman hands! If it gets cold, use a spoon of the appropriate size.

Cooking

If the profiteroles are cooked in too hot an oven, they will rise very quickly and the outsides will burn leaving the insides soggy; they will also collapse when they come out of the oven. If this happens, do not try to recook them, as they will then become rock hard. Do not try to stuff them either as they will probably disintegrate.

Profiteroles emmerdées. Spongy... the way they like them in Provence.

Instead, pile your filling in the middle of the serving dish and stick the profiteroles all over the filling to create a pyramid effect. Then, either pour a light sauce over them (but one sufficiently cloying to cling to and so disguise the offending profiteroles), or decorate the creation with fresh fruit or praline and nuts. You can also sprinkle it with dark brown or demerara sugar.

Alternatively, make some caramel (a generous amount) and coat each puff in it by using tongs and gently 'tossing' the puffs in the caramel. They will then have a lovely crunchy outside that will contrast well with the soggy insides. This also works with profiteroles that have failed to rise through insufficient beating at the egg stage or too slow an oven. Serve them piled high with cream, crème pâtissière or anything flavoured with a liqueur, preferably orange- or coffee-based.

Overcooked profiteroles, provided they are not totally charred, should be cut in half with a sharp knife (so that they do not shatter) and filled with a fairly soggy filling (like whipped cream) early in the day, so that the filling has time to react on the profiteroles and soften them up!

Letting steam escape

Even perfect profiteroles should be pierced to let the steam escape. If they are large, it is better to cut them in half and remove the soggy middles with a spoon, or they will gradually make the rest of the puff soggy too and ruin all your hard work.

Puff pastry

If you have bought this book you are unlikely to be embarking on puff pastry, but, if you are courageous enough to try, here are a few words of advice!

Method

Read the recipe carefully and follow it exactly. Puff pastry was invented for the meticulous, patient and conscientious cook and cutting corners is *always* fatal. So . . .

Do not rush it. Most recipes tell you to rest the pastry between each roll and turn. Do this, indeed you should leave it in the fridge for up to 30 minutes between each roll – the extra chilling will pay off. Puff pastry is best made when you are already doing some other long job in the kitchen so that the fact that it takes all afternoon to make, let alone cook, does not drive you insane.

Do not try to make it in hot weather. Making puff pastry in a heatwave can defeat the most skilled pastry cook and is fraught with danger for the amateur. If the butter melts, you will get into an appalling, sticky mess and there is no way that you will trap the air between the layers of paste – which is what it is all about.

Rolling and cutting

When you roll, do so with great care so that you keep your rectangle of paste rectangular. If the butter gets off centre and the pastry out of shape, you have no hope of it rising evenly and you will end up with a possibly delicious, but not very professional-looking, range of pastry mountains.

Always cut the paste with a very sharp knife that has been dipped in hot water. This means that you get a clean cut through the layers and do not pull them, thus allowing them to rise (hopefully) straight up. Trim any folded edges for the same reason. The fold will act as a sort of selvedge and will prevent the outside edge rising evenly, so you will end up with a hump-backed *mille-feuille*.

If you are cutting individual *mille-feuilles*, make sure that you do not cut them too narrow. If your rolling and turning has worked, they will rise up with such enthusiasm that they will become taller than they are wide and fall over on their sides. If this happens, you merely cut them in three or four horizontal pieces and rearrange them, top to tail so that the unevenness balances up.

If you are making *vol-au-vent* cases, make sure that you cut your lid down *almost* to the bottom of the paste, it will make it much easier when you are fishing out the soggy bit in the middle. Also, when brushing with egg glaze, do not let the glaze run over the cut or it will seal it and make it very difficult to get your lids off and your middles out. You should remove these as soon as the *vol-au-vents* are cooked and cool enough to handle.

Cooking

Make sure that the oven is really hot. It should start at around 500°F/250°C/Gas Mark 9, and then be turned down after 5 minutes to around 375°F/190°C/Gas Mark 5. If you do not have the oven hot enough to seal the paste, the butter will melt before the flour can absorb it and you will end up with a greasy pond in the bottom of the oven and some very heavy pastry.

Make absolutely sure that the shelf in the oven is sitting as straight as it can. If it is at an angle, the paste will not rise evenly and you will end up with a ski slope.

Keep an eye on it while it is cooking. Because the oven needs to be so hot to get the pastry to rise properly, it is very easy to burn either the top or bottom, or both. A piece of greaseproof paper will normally protect the pastry reasonably well.

Failure or success

Once the pastry is cooked, it will either have totally failed to rise, have risen half what it is meant to, have risen lop-sidedly, or be perfect.

1 *Total failure* If it has a nice shiny top, you could just slice off the top layers of all the bits and combine them to make a collection of *mille-feuilles* or *vol-au-vents* cases.

Alternatively, you could put your filling, whatever it is, in the dish and sprinkle the broken remnants of your pastry artistically over the top – this can look surprisingly good.

As a last resort, you could go to the corner shop and buy some ready-made.

2 *Half risen* You should be able to slice it horizontally and scrape the soggy unrisen bits out of the middle. You may still be able to 'stretch' what you have left. Again, use it as a lid rather than a container.

3 *Lopsided* Cut the pastry horizontally and rearrange the pieces top to toe. Once it is filled, no one will ever know the difference. This applies particularly to *vol-au-vent* cases, where the filling will normally hold the case together anyhow.

4 *Perfection* Pour yourself a large drink sit back and admire.

Flaky pastry

Flaky is a cross between shortcrust and puff and, therefore, subject to the hazards of both! However, since the fat is added in much smaller pieces, it is much less difficult to roll correctly. All the same warnings and revival strategies apply to flaky as they do to puff – see above.

Wholemeal pastry

The only difference between wholemeal and 'ordinary' pastry is in the flour. As wholemeal is by nature much coarser than white flour, it should not be used for the 'fine' pastes such as puff or flaky, for it will never achieve a 'fly-away' consistency.

For shortcrust pastry, wholemeal can be used exactly as though it were white flour, but it will tend to produce a rather 'bready' texture. If you want to keep the crispness of ordinary pastry but get the texture or flavour of wholemeal, use half white and half wholemeal flour.

Pasta, Rice and Beans

Most of what is thought of as cheap but nourishing food is relatively easy to cook. It is based on 'peasant' recipes and, as long as it is well seasoned and neither over- nor under-cooked, it cannot go far wrong.

Pasta

If you decide to go the whole hog and make your own, the process is simple but calls for plenty of elbow grease to roll out the dough. A hand-worked pasta machine (a sort of miniature mangle) is quite cheap and an excellent investment, as it takes the sweat out of pasta making and ensures a uniform thickness to your strings.

However, if you do not want to get into making your own, you should be able to buy fresh pasta in most reasonable size towns. Surprisingly, fresh pasta makes the cook's life a lot easier. Dried pasta is chewy when undercooked, and when overcooked bears a close resemblance to a nest of albino worms. Fresh pasta needs only a minute or two's cooking but will still be edible if forgotten for half an hour or allowed to boil almost dry, which is more than can be said for its wormy cousin. This is true of all the various shapes and sizes of pasta.

Both dry and fresh pasta have a tendency to stick to themselves as they cook. Cook the pasta in a large saucepan with plenty of water and a few drops of oil. Stir the pot well when you add the pasta to separate the pieces, then cook it at a good rolling boil. If it still clings together when it is cooked, rinse it through well with boiling water to separate the strands and add plenty of butter, which will 'oil' its way between the strands and prise them apart. If the pasta is really glued into a lump, chop it up and serve it in its sauce as a new and interesting shape of pasta. You could even fry the pieces so that you end up with crisp, browned bits of pasta with a sauce. This is also a good way of reviving leftover, cooked pasta – if you ever find yourself with such a thing.

Lasagne has a peculiar genius for sticking to itself, it is all too easy to find oneself with a large square wedge of totally solid paste. To avoid this fate, feed the sheets of pasta into the water separately. If they are already in, a really good ruffle round with a fork may help to separate them. If not . . . you can try to prise the sheets apart with a sharp knife, but it is unrewarding work. Quicker and more satisfactory is to slice the lumps into tagliatelli shapes. With a little luck, when they are only thin slivers rather than large squares, boiling water will prise them apart. You can then use them as you would have done the squares but serve it as 'Lasagne à la tagliatelli'.

Dried pasta is not as flavoursome as fresh; some people cook it in stock to improve matters. Be sure that you have a really well-flavoured sauce and plenty of it. If you are dubious about the flavour of the pasta or the sauce, grate some cheese over the top and stick it under the grill; it may not be in the best Italian tradition but at least the dish will taste of something!

Fresh pasta, on the other hand, has a very delicate and pleasant flavour that should not be killed with too strong a sauce. If it is a good pasta – a spinach tagliatelli, for example – a little cream or butter and some Parmesan should be quite enough.

When making white sauces to go with pasta, such as macaroni cheese, do not make the sauce too thick. A gluey, floury sauce stuck around some tasteless white macaroni is really unappealing. It's better for the sauce to be too thin and for the pasta to stick up through it. You can then put it under the grill with a little cheese or some breadcrumbs and you end up with a deliciously crispy top over a nice, moist base.

Gnocchi

Gnocchi are feared and avoided by non-Italians as a delicacy requiring enormous skill and patience – which is not true. They are merely balls of dough

that are poached rather than boiled and, provided you stick to the proportions in the recipe, there is nothing to go wrong. (The one exception is potato gnocchi for which you must use floury potatoes – unless you want leaden gnocchi.) A food processor is excellent for making gnocchi, as it ensures a smooth, well-mixed dough.

As with any kind of poaching, the water should only move gently. There is nothing to hold the gnocchi together except the flour and the natural gluiness of the potato or semolina, so fast boiling

water will all too easily rip them apart. Do remember that gnocchi swell in cooking, so do not put too many in the pan or they will grow into each other. If they do, remove them with a slotted spoon and cut them apart with a sharp knife.

Should your gnocchi by some mischance fall apart, be leaden, gluey, or fail to cook properly, do not throw them out – you can make an excellent savoury cake out of them. Put a layer of failed gnocchi in the bottom of an ovenproof dish, then a layer of the sauce you were to serve with them, then another layer of mixture and so on. Top it with breadcrumbs and put it under the grill and you will wonder why you wanted to make it into individual gnocchi in the first place!

All fresh pastas freeze well in their uncooked state, but should not be kept more than 4 weeks.

Rice

Rice, used purely as a vegetable, is normally boiled or steamed.

Boiling

The greatest hazard of boiling rice is that you will overcook it into a solid, glutinous lump, which will block up your sink as well as your digestion!

The more processed the rice has been, the more likely it is to get overcooked. This means that it is almost impossible to overcook the unhusked brown rice that you can now buy in most health

you find your pan overflowing with a rapidly swelling mountain of rice, ladle some out into another pan and add more boiling water to both.

Natural rices, like fresh pasta, have an excellent flavour of their own but the processed varieties may need a little assistance. Cook them in stock or add some dried chopped onions or mushrooms to the rice as it boils.

Rices, being natural creatures, vary in texture, so never rely on the cooking time it says on the packet – if it says one at all. Taste the rice until you are satisfied that it is right. If you do overcook it, do not throw it down the sink – it will

food stores. In fact, this takes up to 10 minutes longer than ordinary rice to cook at all. Italian brown rice is also relatively indestructible, whereas the pre-fluffed varieties can turn into pudding with 2 or 3 minutes of overcooking.

Rice, like pasta, has a tendency to stick together as it cooks. Rinsing it under cold water before you start removes some of the floury coating to the grains and detracts from their stick-together-ability. But, provided you cook the rice in plenty of water, stir it well to separate the grains when you put it in, boil it at a good rolling boil, rinse it in boiling water when it is done, and add plenty of butter or oil to 'slither' between the grains, you should have no problems.

Most rices triple in size during cooking, although the pre-fluffed varieties only double, so do make sure that the pan you cook the rice in is big enough. If

block the drains all the way down the street. Do not try to serve it as it is either, but make it into a rice cake or even a rice pudding, where its sogginess may become a virtue. If you are stuck for a vegetable, you could mix it with a can of drained and well-chopped tomatoes, a bit of tomato purée, some seasoning and maybe a few brown breadcrumbs, put the whole thing in an ovenproof dish and stick it under the grill for a couple of minutes. Alternatively, put it in a food processor, season well, add lots of butter and serve it as a rice purée.

Steaming

Steaming is the most foolproof method of cooking rice and can be achieved very simply, if you do not have a steamer, by putting it in a sieve over boiling water and covering it tightly. Steaming rice takes a little longer than boiling, but it avoids any risk of the rice becoming waterlogged. It is also an excellent way to reheat rice that has got a bit cold or is left over from a previous meal. Indeed, it often pays the harrassed hostess to cook her rice ahead of time and merely steam it hot again when she needs it – one less temperamental pot to deal with when the guests are hammering on the door.

Braising

Even if the rice is to be served as a vegetable rather than part of a dish such as a paella or pilaff, it can be simmered in a smaller quantity of water, which it will absorb completely in the course of cooking. This is the method used with all risottos and pilaff dishes, in which the rice and other ingredients are braised rather than boiled.

In this case, it is as well to fry the rice lightly in oil or butter with the various other ingredients before adding the water – this cooks the floury coating of the grains and prevents the rice sticking to itself. Provided you keep an eye on it, you can then add the water gradually so as to avoid adding too much. If you do add too much, do not try to boil it off or you will overcook the rice. Drain off the excess with a plate or one of those flat sieves designed to stop fat flying around, or suck out some liquid with a bulb baster.

If you add too little liquid, your rice may burn and stick to the bottom. This will not normally matter too much – as long as it is not a blackened ruin. Stir it around well and add more liquid; the burnt bits will merely add tang and texture to the rice. You could also add some finely chopped mushrooms or black olives – they will mingle very 'disguisingly' with the burnt bits of rice!

Beans

Thanks to their 'rough' and nutritional values, dried beans and peas have suddenly rushed back into fashion. They are also very cheap, filling and, if cooked properly, extremely flavoursome.

The basic rule of thumb is that the drier and older the bean or pea, the longer it is going to take to 'soften up', either by soaking or cooking. Since there is no way of knowing how long your beans or peas have been sitting in their bag on the shelf, quite apart from how long it took to get them from the plant into the bag, it is wise to assume that you will always have to soak them.

The slow way of doing this is to soak the beans in cold water for anything from 6 to 36 hours. The quick way is to put them into cold water, bring them slowly to the boil and then simmer them until they are just beginning to soften. At this point, take them off, drain them and start to cook with them – preferably allowing a long, slow cooking process during which they can absorb all the juices and flavours of whatever they are to be cooked with. This pre-boiling could take 5 minutes for green lentils, or a couple of hours for really antique kidney beans. You simply have to test them every half hour or so.

Should you find yourself with bullet-hard beans and not enough time to do anything about them, you can always substitute tinned. As long as you drain them thoroughly and mix them with well-flavoured juices in the pot, they will be *almost* as good as the real thing, though not quite.

Salting

Do *not* salt the beans until the end of the cooking process. If you add salt early in the cooking, or, even worse, at the soak-

ing stage, you merely vitrify the beans in their hard state and nothing short of an atom bomb will soften them. If this happens, do not throw them out – they will do excellently for weighting down your pastry when baking blind.

Seasonings

Beans take very well to herbs, and a handful or two of dried or fresh herbs in a rather uninspiring bean pot will work wonders. So will a tablespoon of tomato paste, some red wine dregs, or even a little Worcestershire sauce.

Dumplings, Quenelles and the Batter Family

Dumplings

Dumplings, or knodel, are a very neglected form of 'vegetable' or 'filler up of empty stomachs'. They are extremely easy to make and can come to grief only if they (like gnocchi or quenelles) are cooked in fast boiling liquid, when they will disintegrate.

However, they must be well flavoured because they do not spend long enough in the casserole or soup with which they are to be served to absorb much of its flavour. Well-textured and well-flavoured brown breadcrumbs, well-flavoured fat – butter or beef suet – mixed with plenty of herbs and seasonings, plus the odd raisin, if you wish to be dashing about it, will make delicious dumplings. They do, however, need to be bound together, but 1 or 2 eggs should be quite enough.

Mix the dumplings by hand so that the seasonings and binder get well distributed. If they are to be small dumplings, make sure they really are small – walnut sized. They do swell as they cook and the larger they are, the more chance there is that they will split open and fall apart.

If you want to make just one large dumpling, wrap it in a piece of muslin or a clean tea cloth and tie the end exactly as for Christmas pudding.

If you are making just one big dumpling wrapped in a cloth, the speed of cooking is not quite so vital, although if boiled too fast it may disintegrate when the cloth is removed. However, with smaller dumplings, it is essential that (like gnocchi or quenelles) they are only poached. If, perchance, they do fall apart, scrape the bits out of the pot as efficiently as possible with a slotted spoon or skimmer, squeeze as much liquid out as you can (put them in a colander and push down with a wooden spoon or spatula) then pile them in a separate dish and serve them as though they were mashed potato. If you have time, put them, uncovered, in an oven for 20 minutes. This will dry the mixture out slightly and crisp the outside. If you then call it a 'Baked Pudding', your guests will be totally unsuspecting and probably even compliment you on the inventiveness of your cooking.

If you do not want to cook the dumplings in a casserole or soup, they can work well as an alternative to potatoes. In this case, cook them in a good home-made stock to add flavour. If they end up completely flavourless, your only hope is to serve them with a 'vigorous' sauce – unless of course what they are accompanying is already so 'vigorous' that you are glad of the dumpling's anonymity!

Quenelles

Quenelles have acquired the same aura of *haute cuisine* as gnocchi but, especially since the arrival of the food processor, they really are very easy to make.

Experts may tell you that a quenelle based on choux paste is lighter and more delicate than one made purely from puréed fish or fowl, egg white and cream. However, it is also less reliable and more likely to disintegrate in the cooking. The egg white, cream and purée mixture, with a good blast in the food processor and half an hour in the fridge before you cook it, will ensure a quenelle that will survive considerable maltreatment. As with gnocchi, gently simmering water is quite sufficient. As a safeguard, butter the poaching dish first, put the quenelles in the bottom and gently pour the water around them.

Do not overfill the pan, as they will swell and collide with each other. If they do, remove some into a second pan with a slotted spoon.

Once they are cooked, they will automatically turn over. You should leave them a minute or two more, then remove them with a slotted spoon and drain them well.

If they should by some mischance disintegrate: scoop the whole lot out, drain it well, add a little more seasoning or flavouring, or the sauce that you had been going to pour over the top, put the mixture in a dish, chill it and serve it as a mousse or pâté.

If you do not drain quenelles thoroughly, or if you pour the sauce over them too soon after removing them from the poaching pan, you will end up with quenelles and sauce floating in a lake of muddy water. The quenelles continue to 'leak' for some time after they come out of the water so leave them to drain on paper towel, or covered in a slow oven until just before you serve them. Then transfer them into a serving dish and pour the sauce over at the last minute. If you do find yourself in the watery-lake situation, suck out as much of the water as you can with a bulb baster and conceal the rest with parsley/watercress/lemon or whatever is to hand. If your sauce is reasonably thin, you may be able to gently amalgamate the sauce and the water in the bottom of the dish.

Quenelles usually err on the side of tastelessness, so do make sure that you have a well-flavoured sauce to go with them. The usual flavour enhancers – tomato paste, curry paste, Worcestershire sauce, herbs, wine, sea salt and black pepper – will all help if you do not have time to start from scratch.

The batter family

Fritters

Except in fish and chip shops, fritters are seldom seen these days, but a crisp, hot, apple or banana fritter can be mouthwatering. However, crisp and hot are the essential elements.

Always ensure that the batter is well beaten and not lumpy. If at all possible, make it in a food processor (best of all), a liquidizer (very good), or a mixer (good), rather than by hand. It should never be too thick – a light 'coating' consistency (like custard or single cream) is quite enough for most fritters, especially fruit ones. If you want a light batter, use some water in the mixture (if you are using beer that counts as water); a batter made entirely with milk can be heavy.

Batter can be used as soon as it is made, but, to be on the safe side, leave it to rest for half an hour. This allows the starch to swell in the flour and ensures a more even and rapid cooking.

Always cook the fritters in hot and *clean* fat – dirty fat will leave a nasty taste on anything. Better an overcooked and slightly burnt fritter than a soggy and undercooked one. If it is soggy and undercooked, return it to the fat and cook it some more, or, if you have already thrown out or put away the fat, put the fritters on a rack in a hot oven. This will crisp them up quite well. Fritters can also be reheated this way.

Batter puddings

To most people, batter puddings mean Yorkshire pudding and variants there-
on. Despite all the dire warnings that 'no one can cook Yorkshire pudding the way that Mother used to', the only things that can ruin a Yorkshire pudding are too heavy a batter or too cool an oven.

The principle on which the pudding works is that the air incorporated into the batter when it is made, together with the egg and flour in the batter, expand very quickly in the heat of the oven, puffing up the pudding. Meanwhile, the fat greases the sides of the tin to allow the pudding to rise and virtually fries its bottom as it does so.

To get a light batter always use half water to half milk. And, before putting the pudding in the oven, ensure that both the oven and the fat in the tin are very hot. If the fat is cold, it is merely sucked into the batter instead of 'frying' the bottom of the pudding.

If, despite all, your pudding fails to puff up and crisp itself, whip it out of the oven, cut it in slices and fry or grill the slices till they are crisp. Then serve them with the meat as 'sippets' – an old English dish ALWAYS served with roast beef.

Pancakes

For disaster-prone cooks, pancakes are such a convenience for the disposal of their disasters that it is worth their learning to make good ones.

The secrets are thin batter and a very hot, nonstick pan. A food processor is the best gadget for batter making, although a mixer or liquidizer will do nearly as well. If you use a food processor, you will not need to rest the batter; nor will you need to remove the lumps. If you do make the batter by hand and manage to create the odd lump, just strain it out before you use the batter.

The consistency should be 'light coating', like a fritter batter, unless you are trying to make American breakfast pancakes, which need to be thick and solid. Most cookery books tell you to use a ladle to pour the batter into the pan, although some people find a jug easier. You will need to experiment to see which you prefer.

It is essential that your pan is absolutely clean. It should be cleaned, cared for and prepared exactly like an omelette pan – see page 35. It should need only the lightest coating of oil or butter between every second or third pancake to prevent sticking. A little melted butter in the pancake mixture also encourages 'slither'. A pastry brush with a little pot of oil is a good way of greasing the pan – although it does not do much for the pastry brush. An alternative is a layer of muslin or a clean cloth wound around the end of a wooden spoon and dipped in the melted butter or oil.

The fat or oil should be really hot before you put in the batter. Drop a little water in the pan to test: if it vanishes it is too hot; if it boils it is not hot enough; if it spits and bounces it is just right.

Pour the batter into the middle of the pan and then, with a neat flick of the wrist, persuade it to run in a thin layer all over the base of the pan. The first few pancakes may well be odd shapes or stick slightly, but once the pan gets hot and well greased (and you get the knack) they should be perfect!

Do allow them to cook on the first side (they are done when they bubble up) before trying to hike them up or turn them over. If you do it too early, you only weaken the structure and they may well disintegrate when you do turn them.

If the pancakes insist on sticking, fail to remain in one piece, or are thick and leaden, abandon the first couple and

They look suspiciously like abandoned pancakes.

plough on. If they continue to be uncooperative, make them anyhow, then fry them lightly in some butter till they are crisp (it doesn't matter what shape they are) and make a layer cake with them and the filling that you were intending to put in them. If the filling is fairly solid, you can do it like a cake; if it is runny, then make it in a soufflé dish. If the pancakes are to be served hot, sprinkle some cheese or breadcrumbs on top and crisp under the grill; if they are to be served cold, decorate the top as though it were a mousse.

When you are stuffing pancakes, if possible do so when the stuffing is cold. If it is hot, it will refuse to remain inside the pancake, the pancake will be impossible to move into its dish, and you will probably burn your hands.

If you are making crêpes suzettes (which, once you have mastered the pancakes, are extremely easy and very impressive) and your brandy refuses to light, it means that you either do not have enough brandy or that it is not hot enough.

The brandy should be heated – but not boiled, which evaporates the alcohol – separately from the sauce. Otherwise it will get drowned in the sauce and refuse to catch light. It should then be lit as soon as it hits the sauce, before it gets a chance to disappear. If the brandy has already gone in, heat *a little* more, light it and add it to the sauce. It will give just enough boost to what is already in there for it all to go up. Do *not* get overenthusiastic with the brandy or you will set yourself alight as well as the dish.

Fish and Shellfish

As fishermen and fishmongers the world over are always telling us, fish is delicious, nutritious, cheap (well, some of it) and easy to prepare – and they are right. It is even pretty disaster-free as far as the cook is concerned, as most fish are happy with the simplest of treatment. Inevitably, there are the *haute cuisine* areas where the disaster-prone should tread warily – for example, dressing a crab demands a certain degree of cool determination. But the majority of fish that comes off fishmongers' slabs or, so often these days, out of the freezer, makes very few demands on the cook.

Smoked, salted, pickled and soused fish

Smoked fish

The simplest fish to serve is a smoked fish, which, theoretically, requires no more than putting on a plate, and surrounding with bits of lemon. However, it is unnerving how often expensive smoked salmon or trout can disappoint by being tasteless, salty or dry.

If an inferior breed of salmon has been used, the flavour of the smoked fish often leaves much to be desired. Serve it with mock caviar, which has a strong flavour of its own (and will make you look as though you are trying even harder), or a well-flavoured soured cream dressing. If it really is tasteless, turn it into a pâté, to which you can add flavour with butter, lemon juice, tabasco, black pepper, or whatever else your supply cupboard offers.

If the smoked salmon is salty (which happens if it has been kept longer than it should have been or if it is frozen), you can try soaking the slices in milk for a couple of hours and then drying them carefully. Alternatively, serve it with a bland mayonnaise or Hollandaise rather than the traditional lemon juice (which emphasizes saltiness). You could also make the slices of salmon into cornets or rolls and fill these with soured cream or a bland creamy filling which will again dilute the saltiness. If the salmon is not too bad, you could serve it actually on brown bread, spread with *un*salted butter, rather than just serving it with it. However, if it is really unpleasantly salty, you will have no option but to turn it into a smoked salmon pâté or mousse – or give it to the cat! If you choose to turn it into a pâté, make sure you use unsalted butter; if a mousse, the cream and eggs in the mixture will do the trick.

Smoked trout are seldom salty but they can be dry. If so, bone them and, rather than serving them with an accompanying sauce, make a horseradish or mayonnaise cream and lightly coat the fish with it. The same treatment can be applied to smoked eel, but in that case you should remove the tough skin as well.

Because of the natural flavour and oiliness of the fish, smoked mackerel are seldom either tasteless or dry. However, if they are, apply the same treatment to them as the others.

If dry or past their first youth, kippers should be soaked for a couple of minutes in boiling water to plump them and then be put under the grill with a good painting of butter till they are almost charred. However, a good kipper should need no more than grilling.

Salted fish

Salted fish does not often come the way of twentieth century cooks, but if it does, it needs very long soaking with frequent changes of water – approximately 48 hours with 8–10 water changes. It then must be cooked slowly, pounded in a pestle and mortar, and mixed with a good deal of cream to achieve edibility. You might well think it wise to avoid this altogether!

Pickled or soused fish

Pickled or soused fish has already had all that can be done to it done before it comes within your grasp. However, be careful not to serve too much of the pickling liquid with the fish as it is normally very strong. It is as well to have a good supply of wholemeal bread or boiled potatoes to soak up the acidity.

Fresh fish

Most good cookery books give comprehensive instructions on how to judge whether a fish is fresh – bright eyes, glistening skin and scales, firm flesh that resists when you press it. However, if you find yourself with a fish that does not comply with these criteria, what do you do?

If it is a shellfish and you are at all suspicious – it does not smell too good, for example – you should throw it out. There is nothing more unpleasant than shellfish poisoning. What is more, many people are to some degree allergic to shellfish and, should one of your guests be of their number, you could make them quite seriously ill. (For oysters and mussels, see pages 77 and 78).

If it is a flat or round fish, make sure that it has been thoroughly cleaned – smell can often be caused by some of the gut being left inside. Soak the fish for 10 minutes in a mixture of vinegar and water and then wash it thoroughly under cold running water. If it still smells, throw it out; otherwise go ahead and use it immediately. The fish will not taste as good as it would have done if it were fresher, but it is unlikely to do you any harm.

Most fishmongers are very willing to clean, fillet and skin fish for you. However, should you find yourself faced with the job (and for some people that might be the greatest disaster they could meet with), take your courage in both hands – it is not nearly as bad as gutting a chicken! Most good cookery books will give comprehensive instructions as to how it should be done. And, if you reduce the fish to a tattered remnant of its former self in the process of skinning or filleting it, do not worry. You can always disguise it with the sauce.

If you are using a slightly elderly fish, it is better to poach than to grill it, and it should be dropped straight into boiling water which should then be reduced to a simmer rather than being brought gradually to the simmer as normal. This way any harmful bacteria that may lurk in the flesh are killed immediately before they have time to work their wrath.

Salmon

Salmon is the one fish that non-fish-minded cooks find themselves faced with at party time. Whether you opt for baking or for poaching, all the remarks about big fish on pages 74–75 will apply. However, there are a couple of points directly relevant to salmon.

One is that in a very fresh salmon there is a creamy curd that extrudes from between the flakes of the fish. Some cooks do not like it and wait a couple of days to cook the fish, by which time it will have disappeared. If you cannot wait, you can, laboriously, scrape it off, but the curd does guarantee that the fish is fresh.

The other point is that, even more than with smaller fish, it is easier to skin a salmon when it is still warm. As it cools, the skin fixes itself firmly back onto the flesh. It is then difficult to remove tidily – and tries one's patience out of all measure! Decoration can, of course, be persuaded to cover the mess but...

Frozen fish

Like it or not, the majority of fish that most of us eat today has been frozen, whether we buy it that way or whether it has been defrosted before it is sold to us. You should, therefore, never refreeze fish that you buy before cooking it unless you are absolutely sure that it is fresh. You will be able to tell if it has already been partially or wholly defrosted as there will be a small puddle of melted and refrozen liquid in the bottom of the bag.

When you do defrost frozen fish,

especially shellfish, keep the defrosted juices and use them in your dish. Fish, especially the smaller shellfish, do lose flavour in the process of freezing and at least some of that flavour is to be found in the frozen juices. If you are using the large shellfish – king prawns or crab claws – make sure that they are really well defrosted and dried. Laid out, attractively decorated, on a platter and served with panache, they can deceive even the most discerning guests.

Some of the cheaper frozen fish come in blocks that are not always, but can be, as tough as old boots. There is really nothing you can do with them except pound them or liquidize them and turn them into a mousse, soufflé or sauce – or give them to the cat.

Grilling

Most fresh, and I mean really fresh, fish are excellent grilled, but you should protect them by painting them with butter or oil or tossing them lightly in flour or oatmeal. Lean fish with a low fat content (sole, for example) should be continuously basted with butter as they cook. Do not salt any fish, as that draws out the flavour, which is just what you do not want to do. If you are cooking the fish whole (rather than opened), slash the skin lightly so as to allow heat to penetrate.

To know whether the fish is cooked, gently raise the flesh from the bone. If it comes away easily and is opaque, the fish is done. It is difficult to overgrill a fish – it just gets a crispy, burnt outside. However, if you do and the fish ends up dried

and frizzled, disguise with the ever handy sauce. Remember to grease the grill pan or rack or you may lose some of the fish as it clings lovingly to it.

There are some dense and dry fish, like tuna or swordfish, that do not take kindly to grilling; it toughens and dries them further. If you do want to grill this

sort of fish, always serve it with a sauce. If the fillets become very tough and leathery, it is better to flake them before serving and to coat them with the sauce, thereby disguising their bootlike consistency. If they are really uneatable, process them and use for fish cakes, pâté or mousse.

Very oily fish, like herring or mackerel, are improved by being tossed in, or painted with, oatmeal or mustard to absorb some of the oiliness.

Frying

Sadly, to many people fish only exist as deep-fried slabs of white flesh wrapped in soggy orange batter. Yet a well-deep-fried fish (an Italian *fritto misto*, for example) can 'delight the palate', and will send a fish freak into raptures.

Deep-frying involves a lot of hot oil and a certain amount of smell, which is why many cooks are anxious to ban it from their kitchens. However, if you are meticulous about keeping your oil clean and if you have some form of smell extractor, the smell can be almost totally eliminated. And, with care, the dangers of hot oil can be minimized.

The most important thing is never to allow the oil to come into contact with the flame or naked heat source. So take great care not to splash the oil and *never* cook too many pieces at the same time. If you do, the oil will froth up and overflow the pan. To avoid this, always use a pan that is rather larger than you need. (See page 13 for what to do if the oil does catch fire.)

In culinary terms, fried fish disasters are rather less cataclysmic. The fish to be fried must always be coated in a protective layer – its own skin, egg and breadcrumbs, a batter, or whatever you choose. If it is not, the juices and flavour of the fish will be sucked out of it by the hot oil and the water content of the fish will turn your deep-frying pan into Dante's inferno.

However, the layer should not be too thick or you will never cook it crisply – or, by the time it is crisp, the fish inside will be cooked to a pulp. It is quite hard to overfry your pieces of fish, provided you do not go off and leave them. As long as the fat is hot enough to sizzle when the fish is dropped in, the fish should be cooked by the time the coating is crisp. But it is easy to undercook not so much the fish as the batter or breadcrumb coating.

If you do undercook the outside layer, you can return it to the pan for a second quick cooking before it is served. Or it can be spread out uncovered on a dish or rack in a moderate oven – this dries up and crisps the outside well. If you want to do the actual frying job beforehand and dispose of the smell and mess, you can quite successfully heat up the deep-fried fillets in the oven some hours later, although purists would claim that they are not – quite – as good as when they are freshly cooked. Incidentally, do not try to be clever and heat them in a microwave. You will get a burnt bit of fish inside an even soggier jacket of batter. They need the dry heat of a conventional oven to cook them properly.

Shallow-frying, by contrast, really is the simplest thing in the world – provided that you grease the pan well before you start. This is especially important if you are cooking a large and heavy fish, which will cling, limpet-like, to an ungreased pan. Use clarified or unsalted butter if at all possible, as the impurities in ordinary butter mixed with the juices that are exuded from the fish combine to make an extremely efficient fixative!

If the fish does fuse itself with the pan, work very carefully and gently with a fish slice and you can usually prise it off. In this case, serve it directly onto the plate rather than a serving dish so that it does not need to be moved again, and decorate with some strategically placed parsley or lemon.

Baking or roasting

Baking in a foil package is the other foolproof way to cook fish. Wrapped in well-buttered foil and cooked in a moderate oven for 8–12 minutes to the pound/450 g (plus 15 minutes for the heat to penetrate the foil), fish is protected from life's troubles and woes – and the cook's mishandling!

With larger fish, such as pike or salmon, it is possible to roast them uncovered or to spit-roast them (well bound to the spit!), but in either case they must be continually and very well basted to prevent them drying out.

Remember that if the fish has been stuffed, it will take a little extra time. However, if it is not cooked when it should be, there is nothing to stop you just putting it back in the oven until it is. Do not try to serve it underdone. Whereas beef and lamb have their attractions 'saignant', a salmon does not. It is better to give the guests another drink – or add another course to the dinner by whipping out some frozen soup or one of your many standby dishes, while the fish finishes itself off.

If, on the other hand, the fish is overcooked, it will be murder to serve but, provided that it has been kept moist in its foil wrapping, its flavour should not have suffered. However, you would be wise to abandon any fancy notion of serving at the table and serve it in seclusion where you can cover the signs of disintegration with sauce, parsley, watercress or lemon.

If you find yourself with a fish that is too large to fit in the oven, cut it in half, cook the halves and then rejoin the fish on the serving dish. It is quite easy to disguise the join, especially if it is to be served cold!

Always try to skin the fish before it cools. If you gently insert the point of a sharp knife under the skin and peel it back, it should part from the flesh quite readily. If it does get cold and proves recalcitrant, you may cause less damage to the flesh by scraping the skin off gently with the back of a knife than by trying to peel it.

Poaching and boiling

Fish should, strictly speaking, never be boiled. The lightest simmer will cook a fish, whereas boiling will break up the delicate flesh and toughen or waterlog what it does not break up. The only exceptions are slightly elderly fish that you wish to 'secure' with a 'quick boil', shellfish (see page 78), and slices of fish. These need to be dropped into boiling water to seal in the flavour and juices and then the water should immediately be reduced to a simmer. All other fish should be put in warm, slightly acidulated water (lemon juice or wine helps to firm the flesh), brought gently to the simmer, and cooked for between 8 and 12 minutes to the pound/450 g, as for baking.

If you do boil or overcook – and thereby disintegrate – your fish, remove it very carefully with a slotted spoon and drain it. Then, depending on how badly it has disintegrated:

1 Reform the shape of the fillet or fish on each plate and decorate with taste and

discretion to disguise where necessary.

2 Use your vegetable, if it is suitable, as a base on which to arrange the pieces of fish artistically and mask them with sauce and decoration. It might be worth making up some instant potato (heavily dosed with cream and butter) to use as a base for the fish, even if you serve very little of it.

3 Whisk out some frozen prawns, artichoke hearts, or anything relatively solid that would blend with the fish, and heat them. Then arrange them tastefully in layers with the fish and coat with sauce.

4 Alternatively, you could convert the fish into quenelles, a mousse, a soufflé, a pie, fish cakes, soup, sauce, omelette or pancake filling.

The disintegration process is, of course, more likely to happen with fillets than with a whole fish. However, a whole fish, if overcooked, may be more difficult to deal with. If the bones are still in it, they can make the flesh taste bitter. In this case, there is not much you can do except serve it with a piquant – or powerful – sauce, which will disguise the bitterness: the inclusion of anchovy essence, chilli, tabasco or mustard would help. However, if the taste is really bitter, there is nothing you can do except offer it to cat.

If you want to cook a large fish and do not have a fish kettle, wrap it in a piece of muslin or a tea cloth (as you would a Christmas pudding) or some foil, and lower it into a saucepan. As with baking, if you do not have a big enough pan, cut the fish in half, cook the halves in separate pans and then rejoin them. However, you do need to raise and lower the fish with care so you don't disfigure the edge which is to be rejoined. If you do not have pans big enough even to do this, put the fish in a baking dish, cover it with the cooking liquid and then with some muslin or a clean cloth soaked in the liquid and bake it in a moderate oven. However, you must ensure that the cloth remains soaked, so as to achieve a cross between poaching and steaming. In each case it will take 8–12 minutes to the pound/450 g.

An alternative, and very easy, way to poach a large fish is to put it in a pan of cold water, court-bouillon or wine and water, bring it to the boil very slowly, then immediately turn it off and allow it to cool in the liquid. By the time it is cold it will be cooked.

Made up fish dishes

Many recipes for cooking fish, especially if it is to be stuffed, involve pre-cooking the fish and then masking with a sauce. The only problem likely to arise in the initial stages is the propensity of your neat little rolls of fish and stuffing to fall apart when you take them out of the pan. Since they are nearly always to be coated with a sauce, a judicious bit of rearrangement will deal with that.

As the fish will continue to extrude liquid after they come out of the oven, it is wise to leave coating with the sauce until the last moment, so that you can drain the fish really well – globules of sauce floating in a watery lake of fish stock do nothing for your reputation as a chef. The best way to avoid this is to store the fish on a rack. Set this over a dish, cover it well so that the fish cannot dry out, keep warm in the oven and only transfer the fish to the serving dish just before you coat them with sauce.

However, if your rolls are in danger of falling apart, you will not want to move them more than necessary. In this case, just before you serve them put a plate as near the size of the dish as you can find over it and drain as much liquid off as you can. If it is too late and the sauce is already swimming in stock, you will be reduced to disguising it with strategically placed watercress — better than lemon as it spreads further — although you could try sucking a bit of the liquid out with a bulb baster.

Do remember when making sauces for fish that most fish (with odd exceptions like mackerel or tuna) are delicately flavoured and need careful saucing. Too rich and creamy a sauce will just kill them. A hint of sharpness from lemon juice, a little cider vinegar, or acid fruits such as gooseberries, will relieve an overrich sauce. On the other hand, you may find yourself with a fish that is so delicate as to be totally tasteless. In that case, you need to disguise the poor thing's deficiencies with a sauce with a good flavour of its own — for example, anchovies, tomatoes, tarragon, or stronger-tasting fish, such as tuna fillets or sardines, mashed and made into a sauce.

Fish cakes and fish pies are unkindly thought of as finny poor relations — only because they are so often stodgy and boring. Fish pies tend to suffer from lack of texture, as the fish dissolves into the sauce which dissolves into the mashed potatoes. Try adding something that has a quite distinct texture of its own — lumps of tuna fish, prawns or mussels; canned corn, artichoke hearts, blanched cauliflower or green beans; or anything else which appeals. And at least ensure that the top is crisp by putting it under the grill, maybe with some cheese, if you are a bit light on flavour, or sprinkle some breadcrumbs over the top of the pie before it goes in the oven.

Fish cakes have a tendency to be leaden — try a mixture of half breadcrumbs and half potato and add a whisked egg white to lighten them. They can also include different bits of vegetable — preferably cooked — to vary their texture, although the more bits that go in, the more likely they are to disintegrate. They should be really well fried in butter so that they become nice and crisp. They can be successfully reheated and crisped, uncovered, in the oven, like fried fish, but in this case put them in a hot oven as you want to crisp the outside without drying up the middle. A good sauce is an enormous help to fish cakes — a flavoured mayonnaise making a pleasant change from tomato ketchup.

Shellfish

The price of shellfish being what it is, none but millionaires or fish freaks are likely to have too many problems with the more exotic molluscs or crustaceans. But in case fortune should one day smile and deposit two dozen oysters and a couple of large lobsters on your doorstep . . .

Oysters

Oysters, theoretically, are the easiest things in the world to serve, as you eat them raw – always presuming that you can get into them! To achieve this, you need a very strong, short knife with a

blunted point (a broken knife is ideal if you do not have an oyster knife) and a thick leather glove. Failing the latter, use a tea cloth, but a leather glove is much better armour against both the oyster and the knife.

The oysters must be cleaned before you start. This involves scrubbing and scraping to remove all debris and ensuring that they are fully shut and, therefore, alive. Operate over a bowl so that you catch all the juices from the oysters as they open. Insert the edge of the knife into the hinge of the shell and

turn to force the oyster open. Then cut through the hinged muscle and run the knife around to open the shell. Which all sounds easy until you try. If you fail or are in danger of amputating your hand, heat the oven to 400°F/200°C/Gas Mark 6 and put the oysters in for 5–7 minutes, then drop them in iced water. This violent treatment should persuade them to succumb to your blandishments.

NB Do not tell any enthusiasts who are to share your feast what you have done as they might try to tell you that it has ruined the flavour.

The larger kinds of clams can usually be treated like oysters, the smaller ones come closer to the cockle and should be dealt with accordingly.

Lobster

A black and viciously snapping lobster could be even more of a 'turn off' for an inexperienced or squeamish cook. All

good cookery books will give you excellent recipes for preparing and cooking lobster – they will also tell you how to kill it by driving sharp knives through the exact point where the brain is situated. If you have some doubts as to where the head is, let alone the brain, it might be kinder to the lobster to drop it into briskly boiling water, which at least ensures it an instantaneous death. After that, you can follow the instructions for preparing it in relative safety! If it looks a bit mangled by the time you have finished, don't worry as it will be easy to disguise any minor deficiencies with sauce, mayonnaise or decoration.

Crab

Should a crab come your way the same treatment is recommended, as the knife method for crab involves cutting nerves, and, in the case of soft shell crab, cutting out the face! Again, you will have to take your courage in both hands and follow the instructions for dressing. For what it is worth, in inexperienced hands a carefully wielded hammer is often more effective than lobster pincers in trying to break into the claws and through the shell.

Mussels, cockles, etc.

Mussels, cockles and the smaller molluscs are easy and rewarding to cook as long as you make quite sure that they are alive when you start. As I said before, shellfish poisoning is not a fate to wish on your worst enemy – let alone your husband's boss! Like oysters, they need to be very well washed under running water both to remove sand from inside and barnacles from outside. The 'beards' which protrude should then either be pulled out or cut with a pair of scrissors. To ensure that the mussels or cockles are fresh, agitate the water so that they close for protection. If any shell seems reluctant to close, take it out and give it a brisk tap with the knife handle. If it does not close immediately throw it out. These shellfish can then be treated like lobsters and crabs and tossed into the boiling cooking fluid. They should all be killed instantaneously and should open. If any do not open, do not try to force them but cast them out from the pot.

Prawns or shrimps

Virtually all prawns or shrimps, unless you have access to your own fishery, will come to you cooked, so at least you do not have to battle with brains and nerves. However, if they are fresh, you do have to shell them.

There is no easy way to shell a prawn or shrimp. Theoretically, you pull the head off and the body will strip off easily. However, 90 per cent of prawns dislike being separated from their shells so, if the head loses the battle and is dragged from the body, the shell fights a rearguard action and rips the skin from your fingers. Nevertheless, it is worth the effort as a fresh prawn is infinitely better than its frozen relative. Incidentally, never throw out the shells as they are the best possible base for a fish stock.

Frozen shelled prawns and shrimps are a great convenience – especially as they are also cooked. However, they can range from tasteless to shredded cardboard. It pays to splash out on the more expensive breeds that may not have much flavour but will at least have the texture of prawns. Always defrost them in, and try to use, their own juice. Provided their texture is acceptable, help them along with an interesting sauce but not one so strong (bottled prawn cocktail mix) that they totally vanish. Ideally, always use them with another fish that will provide flavour while they provide texture. If you have the misfortune to get the cardboard variety, there is really nothing to be done with them except chop them finely and use them in a sauce, pie, fish cake, soup, etc.

Meat

In the days when most people bought their meat in a butcher's, provided you found a good butcher, buying meat was easy. You told him what you wanted the meat for and he would pick out what you needed from the multitude of bleeding chunks before him. Today, many people shop in supermarkets where the meat has already been packaged and labelled, so if you do not know what the label means you have a problem.

Types of meat

As a very rough rule of thumb, the more expensive the meat is, the better it will be. Better, in this context, means that it will be more tender, not necessarily that it will have the best flavour. The tenderest cuts are taken from the parts of the animal that do not move a lot and therefore, do not develop Popeye muscles. However, these cuts are smaller than those taken from the parts that do move a lot and it follows that they will be more expensive. The illustrations give you a basic idea of what does and does not move on an animal, so that when you get home with your packet of meat you can at least identify whether the meat comes from a muscular bit and needs long, slow cooking or a tender bit and can therefore be successfully roasted, grilled or fried.

Age of animal

The age of the animal also has an effect on the texture. The longer a lamb has spent galloping around a mountain, the more developed its muscles will be and the more cooking the meat will need to fall off the bone. But, even if you do buy from a butcher, you have no way of knowing the meat's age and history.

Hanging meat

Certain meats, beef and game are prime examples, are improved by being 'hung' or matured before they are cooked. Unless you buy from a butcher you trust, you will not know whether or not this has been done. However, do not be fooled by beef which is bright red and succulent. Really good quality, well-hung beef should have a purplish tinge and be well marbled or mottled with fat.

Roasting, grilling, braising, etc

In general terms, tender meat can stand being roasted, grilled or fried. Its texture is such that the fibres do not need to

Opposite: *Three diagrams showing the parts of the animals that move and the various cuts of meat that can be bought – (top) beef, (centre) lamb and (bottom) pork.*

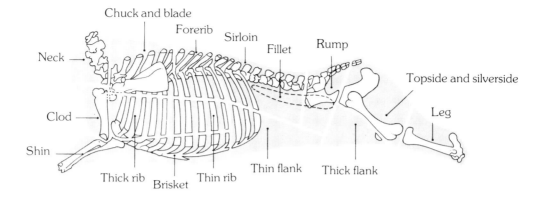

Chuck and blade
Forerib
Sirloin
Fillet
Rump
Neck
Topside and silverside
Clod
Leg
Shin
Thick rib
Brisket
Thin rib
Thin flank
Thick flank

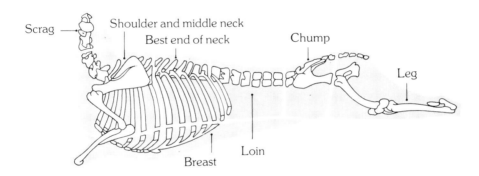

Scrag
Shoulder and middle neck
Best end of neck
Chump
Leg
Loin
Breast

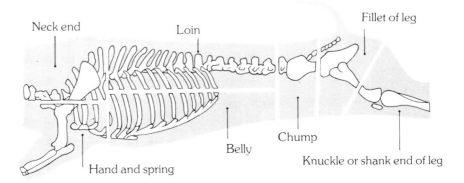

Neck end
Loin
Fillet of leg
Chump
Belly
Knuckle or shank end of leg
Hand and spring

be broken down. However, tough or sinewy meat needs help – if you are not to get lock-jaw through exhausting chewing. The usual way to tenderize meat is by long, slow cooking in liquid (braising, stewing, casseroling or boiling), during the course of which the fibres gradually break down. This sort of dish should be cooked over a couple of days, if at all possible, as it improves both in flavour and texture if it is left to 'rest' for 24 hours after its initial cooking. This is not as time-consuming as it sounds, because once the initial frying processes are completed you can leave it to get on with cooking.

Marinating

If you have what you suspect might be tough meat but you want to roast, grill (barbecue) or fry it, you can break down the fibres before cooking by marinating it. Remember that the more acid in the marinade, the greater the tenderizing effect on the meat, and the longer it is left in the marinade, the more effective it will be. However, marinating also draws out many of the nutritive juices from the meat, so use the marinade to baste the meat as it cooks or to make a sauce for it, which will return the goodness in the juices to the meat.

Salting/pickling

The old fashioned way of marinating, and thereby breaking down the fibres of the meat, was to pickle/salt it. This was a much slower process; properly pickled meat will take anything from 6 to 14 days to achieve. Not many people are likely to pickle at home, but some meats that you buy (pieces of bacon, hams, silversides, etc.) may have been pickled or salted before you buy them. Although salting is no longer nearly as strong as it was in the days when it also had to preserve the meat, it may still be unpalatably so. Always soak any joint that has been salted for 12–24 hours in cold water. If you are worried about it, change the water halfway through the soaking process and replace it with fresh.

Oversaltiness

Most pickled meats are boiled or simmered, so when the pot has come to the boil, check the saltiness of the water. If it is very salty after 5–10 minutes cooking, you would be wise to take out the meat, throw away the water and start again with fresh. The longer the meat cooks in the salty water, the more firmly fixed the salty taste will be. If it is still very salty when cooked, add lots of cream and wads of parsley to the sauce to go with it and serve plenty of beer or mineral water with the meal. Alternatively, serve the meat with strong, sweet pickles – and even more beer or mineral water!

Fattiness

Although fat is shunned with horror by the anti-cholestrol lobby, it is an essential element in good meat both for flavour and moistness. Some meats, like beef, have their fat fairly well-organized: a good marbling through the lean, which forms a natural self-basting system, and a reasonable coating round the outside to prevent it from drying up. Some meats overdo it rather: lamb and pork are very well coated in fat and it is usually necessary to remove some before cooking. Veal on the other hand has virtually no fat and therefore needs to be given some either by larding or barding the joint. This means running extra fat through it with a larding needle or laying fat (usually rashers of fat bacon) over the top to protect it and provide a degree of self-basting.

The amount of fat also depends on the cut of meat. Belly of pork or brisket of beef, which come from the fattiest part of the animal, will have more than their due share, some of which needs to be removed before you cook them. Herbs such as sage and acid fruit – cooking apples, currants, gooseberries, etc. – are good for counteracting the indigesti-

bility of fatty meat. If roasting, use the herbs in stuffings or lay them under the meat; use the fruits as garnish or make a sauce from them. If braising or stewing, add the herbs or fruits to the dish.

Frozen meat

A great deal of the meat we buy is, or has been, frozen, which is not to say that it is not excellent. Meat, both cooked and uncooked, freezes well but you should treat it with a certain amount of care. Check that there are no brown patches of freezer burn on it when you buy it. This indicates that it has been sitting around for some time. When you get it home either put it straight in your freezer, before it has started to defrost, or defrost it and cook it. Frozen meat that has defrosted should not be refrozen without being cooked.

Cooking frozen meat

You can cook meat straight from the freezer but it takes longer and you will lose many of its juices, so it is better to let it defrost naturally first. If you do cook from frozen, depending on how large the piece of meat is, allow anything from 10 to 45 minutes extra cooking time.

Raw meat storage

The larger the piece of meat, the longer it will keep without going off. This means that a roast will be quite happy for 3 or 4 days whereas minced or ground beef should be cooked within 24 hours. It is better to take the meat out of its airtight wrapper before you store it, or at least break the seal so that it can breathe.

Old meat

If, when you come to use it, the meat is a bit whiffy, wash it well in cold water with some vinegar and rinse it several times. If it is still trying to walk out the door on you, it should probably be allowed to do so. If the smell has subsided into a gentle perfume, give the meat one more rinse and use it at once.

Destruction of germs

Any meat, pristinely fresh or grey-bearded and ancient, must be cooked at a sufficiently high temperature to de-stroy harmful bacteria. This is a minimum of 275°F/140°C/Gas Mark 1, if it is to be roasted (although no one in their right mind would roast at such a low temperature); 180°F/100°C if it is to be stewed or braised, since the latter is a more penetrating type of heat. Long cooking at lower temperatures will *not* be the same. In fact, it will make the situation worse, as the bugs will grow and multiply at breakneck speed in the warmth, so that when you come to eat it the meat will be lethal!

An old-fashioned, but very efficacious, way to guard against lurking bacteria is to use sharp fruit sauces, dressings and pickles with cooked meats, as the fruits contain a natural antiseptic which helps considerably to counteract the harmful effects of any remaining bacteria. Serve apple sauce with pork, redcurrant jelly with lamb and game, etc., etc.

Boning

If you have a tame butcher, you will probably persuade him to do any boning and preparation work necessary. Even if you shop in a supermarket, you will find many of the more regular cuts of meat (shoulder of lamb, for example) already boned for you. However, if you do find yourself faced with the task, do not despair. Patience and a sharp, rigid knife are all that you need. Do take care *always* to cut away from you so that if the knife slips it skids harmlessly into the table rather than into your vitals!

The essence of boning any piece of meat is to find the bone and then follow it with your knife, working the flesh away from it as you go. Comfort yourself with the fact that the bones are all inside, so no one is going to see the results of your hacking. Fill up the hole with a good stuffing and tie it into a reasonable shape. A slip knot is invaluable for tying up bits of meat, well worth getting the hang of if you do not already know how.

Roasting

Before you start to roast your meat, no matter what it is, remember that once it is roasted its quality cannot be disguised – or you are unlikely to have enough time to do anything sufficiently radical to disguise its toughness. So be sure that it is a good piece of meat. If at all dubious, go for an alternative method of cooking, such as pot roasting or casseroling the joint whole, see page 87.

Roasting originally meant cooking in front of an open fire; ovens never achieve quite the same effect as they are, by their nature, enclosed; so the heat cannot be as dry as in the open. To get as close as possible to the original, by maximizing the circulation of hot air, cook the roast on a rack over an oven tray. If you are concerned that it could be dry, lay some bacon over the top or baste it periodically with fat or butter – not water as that merely creates steam. Roast veal should be basted frequently. The insertion of slivers of garlic or parsley stalks into a roast of lamb is thought to improve both taste and texture.

Timing

The time it takes to cook a roast will depend on the shape, thickness and age of the meat, the exact temperature of your oven, what else you are cooking at the same time, etc., etc. However, as a rough guideline:

Beef takes 15 minutes to the pound/ 450 g in a hot oven, if you want a rare centre.

Lamb takes 20 minutes to the pound/ 450 g with 20 minutes over in a hot oven, for a pink middle.

Veal takes 20–25 minutes to the pound/ 450 g in a moderately hot oven.

Pork takes 30–35 minutes to the pound/ 450 g in a moderate oven.

'Doneness'

The most foolproof way to know whether your meat is cooked is to use a meat thermometer. This will give you the correct temperatures for the meat to have achieved the right degree of 'doneness'. However, if you do not have a thermometer, use the touch test (firm = well done; soft but resilient = medium rare), or the prick test. Prick the meat until you can see the juices run: red juice indicates rare; pink juice indicates medium rare; colourless juice indicates well done.

Lamb should be pink or well done depending on taste. White meats such as veal or pork must always be well cooked to make them digestible and safe to eat. Pork houses particularly active bacteria that must be killed in the cooking process. The flesh should be white or greyish when it is done. If it is still pink, you must put it back in the oven till it is properly cooked, even if that means giving the guests another drink.

Carving

Carving roast meat is not difficult, as long as one applies logic and a sharp knife. Always stand to carve and cut down rather than across, so that if the knife slips it will plunge itself into the board or dish, not into you. Use a fork with a guard to protect your other hand.

However, always have some garnish, or possibly a thick sauce with lots of 'bits' in it, so that if you do end up with hacked remnants you can disguise them before they get onto the table.

It helps the carver if the roast meat is taken out of the oven for 10–30 minutes before it is to be carved and kept warm. This stabilizes and firms the texture of the meat so that it does not slither, shyly, away from the knife when you start to carve.

Reheating

It is not advisable to reheat roasts, as by the time they get hot they have dried out as well. The only exception is if you have a microwave oven. Because the heat is generated from inside rather than outside, it does not dry out the meat. If you do not have a microwave, either reheat the remains of the roast in some stock in a pan, or slice it and heat it in gravy.

Grilling or frying

As with roast meat, only the best quality meat should be used for grilling or quick frying as it gets no tenderizing in the process of cooking. What is more, you have no way of disguising its toughness once it is done, as it is a last-minute process and should go straight from the grill or frying pan to the table.

To grill or pan fry successfully, you should first sear the outside of the meat under or over a very hot heat to improve the flavour, so always pre-heat the grill or pan. (If frying, you may need a very little fat just to grease the pan.) Then reduce the heat slightly, but remember that the meat does need to be cooked quickly as, if it goes on cooking for too long, it will toughen and dry up. As a safeguard against dryness, have a good sauce, relish or pickle available.

Keep one steak, chop or cutlet (your own) which you can test for 'doneness' by cutting a little slit in it. With the exception of pork, undercook rather than overcook, as an underdone steak or chop can always go back under the grill, whereas an overdone one is irretrievably ruined. The amount of cooking time that each steak, chop or cutlet will need will depend on the thickness of the meat, how close you can get it to the heat source and how hot your grill will get. It would be wise to experiment before wasting expensive fillet steaks by overcooking them. As a very rough rule of thumb, it is unlikely that anything will be done (both sides) in less than 5 minutes, and in 10 most will be reduced to a cinder.

Casserole cooking, braising and stewing

Any kind of slow cooking where the meat is submerged, or partially so, in liquid will be much kinder to it than roasting or grilling. Whether the meat to be cooked is in a large piece or has been cut up, the principles are exactly the same. This slow cooking can either be done in a saucepan on top of the stove (keeping the heat very low so that the contents don't stick to the bottom of the pan), or in a casserole in the oven.

Kind of meat

There can be as much danger in using the wrong kind of meat for braising as for roasting. If you use one of the tender cuts and cook it long and slowly, it will totally disintegrate and you will be left with a deliciously flavoured meat gravy.

If you discover in time you could:

1 Spend a fortune on some more fillet steak, which you could then cut in smallish pieces, cook quickly in some butter and add to the dish.

2 Cheat and take a can of stewed steak or the equivalent from the store, drain off all its juice and heat it through in your delicious sauce.

3 Add a rather more solid canned or frozen vegetable that could get mistaken for meat in the sauce.

4 Brazen it out.

Sealing and browning

There is a long held belief that meat should be seared first to seal it and prevent the loss of too many juices. However, although searing the meat undoubtedly improves the flavour, it is not at all certain that it seals in the juices. The amount of 'searing' required depends on the meat and the dish. Veal to be used in a blanquette of veal should only be fried lightly in a little butter to keep it white; the beef for a bourgignon should be well browned. Ensure that the meat is dry before you fry it, otherwise it will just boil in the juices. If you under-brown the meat, you will end up with an insipid colour to your dish and a certain lack of flavour. Colour can be improved by the addition of a little gravy browning or caramel. Flavour would benefit from well-browned vegetables, sherry or a dash of Worcestershire sauce.

If you burn the meat, it may have a slightly bitter taste – which you could always pass off, as did one quick witted host, by calling your frizzled dish, 'Smoked . . .'.

Cooking

Once the meat is seared, it only remains for it to be cooked long and slowly in flavour-giving juices. Vegetables always lend flavour, as do herbs, fresh if possible, but otherwise dried. Wine will help to break down the fibres in the meat and, as long as it is cooked sufficiently, very cheap or home-made wine will be quite acceptable.

Seasoning

Do not season too early in the cooking, as the flavours develop and concentrate the longer the dish cooks. Ideally, the meat should be cooked 1 or 2 days before you want it so that it has time to 'mature', and then be gently reheated in its own juices before you serve it. If you do overseason, dilute the sauce with some water (not more wine which will only emphasize the saltiness), use plenty of parsley, underseason the vegetables, and make sure that you serve a bland, mopping-up-type vegetable, such as rice or mashed potatoes to counteract the saltiness.

Casseroling lamb and pork

Because both lamb and pork are fatty, they need very good skimming to remove the excess fat. Always cook them ahead of time, so there is time for the meat to cool down and the fat to rise to the surface so that it can be removed. If you do not have time to do this, remove as much as possible with a spoon or paper towel. Alternatively, pour off as much of the liquid as you can into one of those jugs which separate the fat from the juices, then return the latter to the pot. Because of the fat in lamb and pork, they go well with fat-absorbent vegetables, such as dried beans in cassoulet and other bean dishes.

Casserole cooking veal

Veal releases a great deal of scum as it cooks. To minimize this, before you start to cook it properly bring it to the boil in some cold water, simmer for a couple of minutes, then take it out and rinse it under cold water. This will get rid of most of the scum, although you still need to watch it in the early stages of cooking and remove any extra that may appear. If you do not do this, you will just have to skim very carefully, as the scum from veal, although harmless, has a rather unpleasant taste and a thoroughly unappetizing appearance.

Good veal is now so expensive that many people prefer to substitute chicken or turkey in recipes requiring veal. These can be perfectly acceptable alternatives, as the flavours are not dissimilar.

Specific meats and dishes

Escalopes/fillets of lamb, veal or pork

Some of the better cuts of meat are often lightly fried and served with a sauce. Because these are cooked lightly and quickly, the meat needs to be of good quality. One way to break down lurking fibres is to beat or flatten the meat before you cook it. If the butcher has not already done this for you, or if you want to make doubly sure, put the meat between two pieces of greased paper before you start to beat it. If you beat the escalopes naked, they will disintegrate rather than flatten – and stick to your beater. A mallet or the flat of a cleaver work well. If neither is available, a gently wielded croquet mallet would do very nicely.

Do not overcook escalopes, whatever the meat. Because they are so thin, they toughen very quickly and taste like sauced leather. If you do overcook them, slice the escalopes into fingers and serve in their sauce – at least the texture will not be so noticeable.

Veal substitute

If using chicken or turkey breasts in place of veal, they should be flattened like the escalopes.

Colour

If you are working with veal and are not happy about the colour, it can be paled either by blanching it very briefly in boiling water, or by soaking it overnight in milk.

Noisettes of lamb

Because noisettes of lamb are so hideously expensive. it would be a pity to ruin them by bad cooking. They can be fatty, so be sure to remove as much fat as you can during the cooking process and skim the sauce well before you serve it. Despite the fat around the noisette, the kernel of the meat is dry, so serve with a good sauce.

Beef olives

Beef olives are another expensive 'party dish' – they take a lot of preparation and can be ruined by being tough or dry. The stuffing that goes inside the rolls of meat should have a good proportion of fat and the olives should be served with a rich, well-flavoured sauce.

Mincemeat

Once meat is minced or ground, you have no way of knowing what it is you are getting. If the meat is to be used as a base for some highly flavoured and seasoned dish, its quality is not that important – although you should take care as cheap mince is often greasy and should be well de-fatted before being incorporated into the main dish. However, if you want the mincemeat for a hamburger mix or a shepherd's pie, it is going to be on full gustatory view so make sure that it is good quality or buy your meat whole and mince it yourself.

If you are at all dubious about the quality or flavour of the meat, spice it highly. The spices will help to break it down if it is tough and will also, like fruit, act as a built-in antiseptic against whatever may lurk within. Also, cook it very thoroughly so that you are sure to kill any bacteria.

Venison

Once upon a time, venison was a luxury meat that you only met if you happened to know a friendly poacher.

However, today deer are being farmed for meat and, although venison is still expensive, it is readily available.

Although well flavoured, venison is dry and has no in-built fat. It therefore benefits from marinating, even if it is to be roasted, and should also be larded or barded before it is cooked. Young animals roast well, but if you are not too sure of the age it might be wiser to marinate and then braise or casserole the meat. For roasting, it needs approximately

20 minutes to the pound/450 g. If you do roast and then discover that it has climbed several mountain ranges during its life, you could successfully casserole what is left.

Sausages

A small plea for the 'real' sausage. A proper pork sausage, filled with herbs and spices and grilled or fried in a little butter, is a gastronomic delight. Prepackaged, bread-filled, uniform, pink so-called sausages are a DISASTER and should be banned. You can, if you wish, make your own, but just try spending a little more buying them from a good butcher or delicatessen – you will not regret the expense.

Pies

(For pastry problems see chapter.)

It is usually better to cook the contents of the pie before you top it with pastry. Since pastry cannot stand more than around 45 minutes cooking without getting burnt, and most of what is likely to go in a pie needs at least an hour, if they are cooked together something is going to have to suffer.

The contents of a pie can be prepared entirely separately – a chicken fricassée, for example, which is then put in a pie dish and topped with pastry – or they can be cooked in the pie dish (like a steak and kidney pie) then topped and returned to the oven. The extra cooking will not do the meat any harm and you can be sure that you will not overcook the crust.

If it is too late for such niceties, it is better to overcook the crust than undercook the contents. If you fear that is going to happen, cover the pastry with some greaseproof paper or foil, which will protect it and slow down its cooking while not affecting its contents.

Raised pies

Raised pies are a rather different matter as the essence of a raised pie is that the pastry should absorb the flavour of the meat as it cooks. Do not add the juices till after the pie is cooked. If you put them in at the beginning, they will merely waterlog the pastry so that it will be soggy rather than crisp. If you already have added the juices – too late, you will just have to have soggy pastry.

En croûte

Meat served *en croûte* is somewhat in the luxury line and, on the whole, disaster-prone cooks should probably steer clear. However . . .

For a dish *en croûte* the meat should be of the best quality, as it is roasted, rather than stewed or braised, before being encased in pastry and is served, carved, in one piece. However, like a pie, it should be cooked in advance so that the pastry does not burn while the meat is cooking. But take care not to overcook the meat the first time round as it will get cooked again.

Before wrapping the meat in the pastry (which should, if you are doing the job properly, be flaky or puff, but can very satisfactorily be a good shortcrust) make sure that everything – meat, pâté coating and pastry – is well chilled. It is a good idea to add an egg to the pastry which gives it greater tensile strength. Then cook it in a very hot oven – as high as 400°F/200°C/Gas Mark 6 – to make sure that the pastry is sealed and cooked before the heat has a chance to penetrate too successfully into the inside. Always cut slits in the pastry outside after you have decorated it to let the steam escape and brush it very well with beaten egg so that you get a good browned outside. If it manages to stay in one piece, bring it to the table, show it off and then take it away to serve. No matter how perfect, it will disintegrate when carved.

Storage of cooked meat

Most cooked meats will keep 3 or 4 days in a cool larder or refrigerator. Roasts that are to be served cold will begin to lose their colour and flavour after 3 days. At that point, they are still perfectly usable and should be turned into a pie, curry or casserole. Meats that have been cooked and stored in a sauce, especially if it is a spicy one, will normally keep for up to a week in a refrigerator. However, care should be taken if the weather is particularly humid. When the stored meats are to be eaten again, make sure that they are thoroughly reheated to well above 275°F/110°C, so as to be quite sure that any bacteria are killed.

When storing cooked meats in sauces, be they casseroled or minced, never store them in quantities over 2 pints/ 1 litre/5 cups. If in larger quantities, it takes so long for the centre to cool down that it has gone off before it does, thus contaminating the rest of the mixture. You will then be confronted with a heaving mass of meat which can only be consigned to the waste-disposal or the dustbin – not even the cat will have anything to do with it!

If you discover too late, all you can do is to drag out everything you have in the freezer, plus everything you have in tins, tip it all into one large pot, stir and hope for the best. It could be wonderful!

Panic! The fish won't even go in the oven, let alone the dish. Keep calm. Get out a large knife, cut the fish in half to cook, then reassemble it on the serving dish. Overlapping slices of cucumber, radish or tomato will do a great cover-up job.

Opposite: *Sodden, watery and depressed – is that how your Brussels sprouts look? Drain them thoroughly and purée them with cooked Jerusalem artichoke, parsnip, turnip, swede, mashed potato, or even instant mash, and you will be complimented on your delicious and imaginative vegetables.*

Are your meringues flat, cracked, overcooked, stuck to the base, broken? Take heart! Plenty of whipped cream and some tastefully arranged plums or soft fruit and your gâteau will win you a prize.

Poultry, Game and Offal

Poultry and game

Although there are a large variety of game birds available to those who shoot or who can afford them when they appear in upper-crust butchers in early autumn, the only birds that most of us see are endless frozen chickens, a turkey at Christmas and, occasionally, a duck.

Chickens

Since the arrival of a deep freeze in every home, and Colonel Sanders on every street corner, chickens have got themselves rather a bad name. Not only are many of them flavourless and/or tough but, if they are not properly defrosted, they will kill you!

This is rather unfair to the chickens as, although they can be both tough and flavourless, frozen chickens can also make an excellent, cheap and nutritious base for innumerable sauces. Do watch out though for brown patches of freezer burn, which would indicate long, and possibly bad, storage.

Opposite: A champagne sorbet – or a puddle of half-melted snow? Convert it into a refreshing cocktail and serve it as the latest fashion – in the middle of the meal!

Turkeys

Although turkeys still make their star appearance at Christmas they are becoming more and more of a year round bird. Moreover, they are now being sold in portions which make them quite feasible even for one person to buy.

'Keepability'

Fresh poultry will keep for a couple of days in a fridge before it is used. Frozen poultry, if defrosted, should be used within a maximum of 36 hours. When you take poultry out to use, if it is at all smelly, wash it well in vinegar and water. If it remains very smelly, throw it out; if it only retains a delicate scent, cook it at once but be sure that you cook it very thoroughly.

Salmonella

Salmonella is dangerous but, provided that you observe the basic rule that all frozen poultry must be both thoroughly defrosted before it is cooked and thoroughly cooked before it is eaten, you will be all right. This applies particularly to large birds, which can take up to 48 hours to defrost properly and up to 4 to cook thoroughly. (For suspected salmonella poisoning, see page 15.)

Roasting

Roasting any bird, chicken, turkey, duck or game, presents a fundamental problem in that the breast and the legs are different types of meat and it is difficult to cook one correctly without either overcooking or undercooking the other. It does not matter too much with small birds, where the whole process may not take more than half an hour, but with a turkey by the time the breast is properly cooked the legs are dried out and overdone. Added to this, you have the problem that the meat of a chicken or turkey is essentially dry and therefore needs to be larded or barded to keep it moist. So, by the time you have barded its breast and protected its legs with foil or greaseproof paper, the poor bird goes into the oven looking as though it has been in a car crash!

To counteract their natural dryness, cook the large birds the French way, in a shallow bath either of stock or water, so that the steam keeps them moist. Alternatively, wrap the whole thing in foil with lots of butter and seasoning and let it get on with it.

Duck and goose

Ducks and geese are even more contradictory birds as they combine extreme fattiness with rather dry meat. When a bird is to be roasted, you need to release as much of the surface fat as possible by pricking the skin all over so that the fat can escape during cooking. Roast the bird on a rack rather than in a tin, or the fat will run down into the tin and the bird will fry rather than roast. In order to keep the flesh as moist as possible, stuff the cavity with a well-flavoured stuffing. This will prevent the breast drying out from within. To counteract the richness of the meat, use sharp herbs and fruits either in the stuffing or in the accompanying sauce. Never throw out the carcases; they make wonderful soup.

Casserole or pot roasting

Unless you are sure of your bird it may be wiser to casserole roast rather than dry roast. This applies particularly to smaller game birds, which can all too easily be both dry and tough. This is not, though, recommended for duck or goose, as you have no opportunity to release the excess fat. If you do want to casserole one of these, par-roast it first to get most of the fat out.

When casserole roasting, sear the bird lightly all over in hot fat, then settle it in a heavy casserole, not much larger than itself. Add herbs, vegetables as required, stock, wine, brandy or whatever seems appropriate for the bird and cook long and slowly in order to extract maximum flavour and ensure maximum tenderizing.

Carving

Carving birds is not such a terrifying prospect as long as the knife is sharp and you have your wits about you. Remove the leg first – if that is possible. With a large turkey it would need

Tarzan to get its leg off! Then carve your way through the breast. The easiest, though the least elegant, way to cut up the legs, assuming that you wish to divide them amongst the guests, is to take the poultry shears and cut through the joint. If you have to do it with a knife, make sure that the knife is firm and not too long. Get its point stuck well into the joint, then twist. If you are worried, either carve the thing in the kitchen or on a side table where your back is to the guests and they cannot see you pick it up and wrench it apart.

Jointing or boning

Many chicken recipes call for chicken pieces. It is easy, but more expensive, to buy your chicken already in pieces – or you can get your friendly butcher to prepare them for you. But if you are stuck with cutting up a chicken yourself, get hold of a pair of poultry, or *clean*, grease-free garden secateurs, and work your way through the joints. If you have no secateurs, you will have to do battle with a knife, but make sure it is short, rigid, sharp, and pointing away from you. Even if the poor chicken ends up looking rather hacked, it will get disguised in the cooking.

If you want to stuff a boned chicken, do not ask a butcher to bone it unless you are very sure of your butcher. It is a fiddly job which most butchers hate and careless boning will be far worse than none, as you will have to spend hours sewing up the wretched bird's gashes. Take your courage, and a knife, in both hands, slit the chicken down the back and carefully cut away the flesh from the bone wherever you find it attached. It is a great deal easier than you think. If you nick or hack the skin, have a needle and thread handy, so that you can patch it up.

When you get round to stuffing the bird, remember there will be a very large area of space in the middle, which will be cut straight through when it is carved. Arrange your stuffing as though you were making a pâté, with an eye to colour and shape when it is cut.

Boiling, braising or casseroling chicken/turkey

Long slow cooking in wine with herbs and vegetables will improve the flavour of the most uninspiring chicken. 'Long' for a jointed chicken would be 1–1½ hours; even a tough chicken will not take as much cooking to tenderize as a tough piece of beef.

For flavour it is better to leave the bones in, but you may wish to remove them before you serve the dish. If the chicken is really well cooked, the meat will have fallen off the bones anyhow and you will be in danger of dishing up bones with no meat.

Chicken dishes in white sauce

Because of the natural blandness of the meat, white sauces need to be flavoured with care so that the whole dish is not insipid. Do not throw in quantities of salt in desperation. Use some more interesting spices (ginger is excellent with chicken) or lemon juice to give it a tang, or serve a flavoursome vegetable (artichoke hearts, spinach, haricots verts) as part of the dish, or to accompany it, to help the flavour.

Cold chicken

Cold roast chicken can be very dry unless great care has been taken both in cooking and storing it. Unless you are quite sure that it is moist, serve it dressed in a cream or mayonnaise sauce, with a squeeze of lemon juice or a little vinaigrette.

Offal

Whereas most meat is better when matured, offal should always be eaten absolutely fresh. Although pigs' trotters, calves' heads, chitterlings and tripe are not likely to come our way too often, kidneys, liver, tongue, sweetbreads and brains are all rightly thought of as delicacies.

Many of the problems that people encounter with offal have nothing to do with the cooking of it but with the fact that they have bought the wrong kind for the wrong purpose. This applies especially to liver and kidneys.

Liver

Calves' liver is the finest of the livers – tender, juicy and rich. Lambs' liver comes not far behind. Not so pigs' or ox liver, both of which are strong and tough; fine for flavouring casseroles but horrible on their own.

Price will be a guide, as calves' liver is two or three times as expensive as pigs' or ox. If, perchance, you do buy the wrong one and it is too late to turn it into a casseroled dish, cut it up very small, sauté it in some butter, try to find something like mushrooms to put with it, and serve it in a well-flavoured sauce. If you have some wholegrain rice to serve with it, the nutty texture of the rice will distract attention from the chewiness of the liver.

Calves' or lambs' liver, should only be sautéed very lightly in butter; it should first be sealed to keep the juices in, then cooked gently, but not for too long, as overcooking will toughen it. A couple of minutes on either side should be quite sufficient to cook it yet keep the middle pink.

Since it is so rich, it is best to serve it with a piquant accompaniment – a little fried bacon, some cooking apple fried in butter, or a sauce well flamed with brandy.

Kidneys

Veal and lambs' kidneys are the ones to use if you want to grill or sauté them to eat alone. Trim them carefully and remove the core, cutting as little as possible into the kidney, then grill or sauté them lightly till the outside is brown but the inside is still pink. Ox and pigs' kidney, like ox and pigs' liver, is much stronger and should only be used in small quantities with another meat, or when it is to be cooked long and slowly. For example, ox kidney is excellent for steak and kidney pie, where its flavour blends well with the steak and it has enough time to cook gently without getting tough or overcooked.

It is difficult to mistake ox kidney for lambs' or calves' as it is much larger with many lobes rather than the familiar kidney shape. However, should you do so, cut it in thin slices and cook it gently in butter. If it is for breakfast, serve it with a fat, well-grilled tomato or lots of mushrooms to tone it down a bit; if it is for dinner, serve with plenty of vegetables, sauce and rice or mashed potatoes to absorb the strong flavour.

Sweetbreads and brains

You will normally be able to buy both sweetbreads and brains ready cleaned and prepared. If not, soak them in acidulated water, then peel away all the membrane and fibre you can find. It is fiddly rather than difficult. Neither sweetbreads nor brains keep well so they should be cooked within 24 hours of purchase. However, in most places you will get frozen ones that have already been prepared, which saves a lot of work.

Cook them lightly in butter with a light, cream sauce. Since their own flavour is very delicate they should not be killed by strong seasonings. For those who really like them, the best way of all to eat them is cooked in a little butter and served on toast.

Vegetables and Salads

Vegetables

Vegetables today are not only legion but very fashionable. Most are easy to cook, provided that you treat them sympathetically, although inevitably, there are certain rogues.

Freshness

In an ideal world, all the vegetables we eat would come straight from the garden, as there is no doubt that really fresh vegetables do taste very much nicer than elderly ones. However, gardens are not always to hand and we often have to make do with drooping leeks, wrinkled parsnips, soggy tomatoes and all the other nasties that the supermarket offers or our fridge disgorges.

If your vegetables are not as fresh as you might wish, do not attempt to serve them raw. Always cook them (they will have lost much of their nutritional value anyhow through old age) and give them a helping hand wherever possible. Braise them in butter, cook them in a sauce, or sprinkle some grated cheese or breadcrumbs over them and put them under the grill. Whatever you do, do not bare their imperfections to view by merely boiling them and serving them naked. Incidentally, a little sugar added to a slightly 'past it' vegetable will help both its texture and flavour.

Overcooking

Despite the unflagging efforts of cookery writers and vegetable lovers over the last quarter century, cooked vegetables still have a recurring tendency to sogginess. It cannot be shouted loud enough, or repeated too often, that a vegetable is infinitely happier undercooked and slightly crunchy than overcooked, waterlogged and tasteless. There are a couple of exceptions to this rule, but so few as to not even dent its validity.

If, perchance, your vegetables do get overcooked, do not serve them as they are. This applies to root vegetables that have gone mushy, leafed vegetables that are waterlogged and soggy, bulb vegetables, like onions, leeks and celery, that have lost their crunch and texture, tomatoes that have disintegrated, or any other vegetables that look you wearily in the eye and tell you quite clearly that this was not how nature intended them to be eaten.

If the vegetables are that soggy, they will easily mash into a purée (in the food processor if necessary), and dry off quickly in a saucepan. Stick in lots of butter and seasoning and, if necessary, mix another tinned or frozen vegetable into the purée to give it more bulk or interest. Add chopped nuts or sunflower seeds to give some sort of texture, or sprinkle some breadcrumbs over the top and put the purée under the grill for a few minutes.

Certain vegetables such as Brussels sprouts may be rather watery when puréed on their own, so mix them with a puréed root vegetable – mashed potatoes (real or instant) are usually the closest to hand, but other vegetable mixtures can be the gourmet's delight – Brussels sprouts and Jerusalem artichokes, for example, or parsnips and tomatoes.

If you have time, which you probably will not, whisk a couple of egg whites, fold them into the dried out vegetable purée, stick it into a hot oven for 15 minutes and you will have a souffléed vegetable – so the last state of man will be better than the first!

Boiling and steaming

The reason that so many vegetables end up damp and flaccid is the deep-rooted belief that vegetables should be cooked in vast amounts of fast-boiling water. With very few exceptions (beetroots and turnips maybe), the opposite is true. If you must use water at all, an inch/2.5 cm in the bottom of the pan is enough. If you really want to be kind to your vegetables, steam them. This does not involve a large expenditure as a cheap enamel steamer works excellently, as does a colander sitting over a pan of boiling water with some foil or a lid fixed over it.

Steaming takes slightly longer than boiling but it gives the cook a great deal more leeway. A Brussels sprout that will be ruined if overboiled will be quite edible if oversteamed. Most vegetables retain their texture, flavour and colour if left in the steamer with the heat turned off for anything up to 10 to 15 minutes. Even if the vegetable does get overcooked, it will at least not be waterlogged.

Many vegetables can, like rice, be steam-cooked in advance and reheated in the steamer before they are to be served. This practice should not be used too often but can be of great help to the harrassed hostess who is battling with the gravy, or the roast that has got itself immovably wedged in the tin.

Braising

An alternative method of cooking that has great advantages in terms of unruinability is braising in butter, or butter and a little wine. This works particularly well with some of the more watery vegetables like courgettes (zucchini), where you do not want to encourage them to absorb any more liquid than they are already endowed with. Any vegetable, cut into pieces of equal size, browned in a little butter, then covered and cooked very slowly in its own juices, will have an excellent flavour and its texture will become a great deal less important than if it were boiled. However, root vegetables are slow to cook this way. A slightly crunchy or nutty texture in your parsnip is not unpleasant, but you do not want it totally raw!

Baking

Baking root vegetables in their 'jackets' is the easiest of all ways to cook them. But not all vegetables have 'jackets' that improve with baking. Potatoes and parsnips are fine, but a large turnip or sweet potato will need a hatchet to get into it.

If you do bake a vegetable and are dubious about the skin, test one before you serve it. If you find the skin is like elderly leather, cut the vegetable in half, scoop out the flesh, mash it lightly with a little butter and seasoning, return it to the skin and use the skin as a decorative container. If someone wishes to risk his dentures on the skin, their destruction will be on his own head not yours.

A skewer stuck into a baked vegetable does convey the heat into the centre and help to speed up its cooking. Pre-cooking a vegetable for 7 to 8 minutes in a microwave will also speed up cooking, but do leave it long enough in an ordinary oven for the skin to get well browned. If you are desperate, you can crisp the skin under the grill but it is not very satisfactory. If your meat is cooked, your guests are champing at the bit, and your baked potatoes, parsnips, etc. are still rock solid . . . Halve the potatoes, dig out and abandon the middles and return the skins to the oven to crisp up. Serve them with lots of butter, herb butter, cream cheese, or whatever else you can find in the fridge. Vegetable skins are all the rage these days – although they are not much good at mopping up gravy! If you want to add lustre to the skin, you can brush it with oil or sprinkle it with salt, but that is not usually necessary.

It is wise to prick the skin of a vegetable that is to be baked. If the skin is particularly well fitting, the air inside will expand and get trapped. The result is usually a mighty bang as the vegetable explodes scattering its contents all over the inside of the oven! Should this happen, it will depend on the violence of the explosion as to what you can do about it. If the explosion was relative-

ly minor, you should be able to rescue most of the insides of the vegetable, mash them with some butter and seasoning and return them to the skin – maybe with a little decoration on top so that it looks as though you meant it that way! If retrieval of the insides proves impossible, leave the skins to crisp off entirely and serve with lots of herb butter, etc.

Most vegetables, other than root vegetables, (cabbages, fennel, celery, onions, leeks, etc.) take to baking well, but need to be baked in a container usually with a little butter and some seasoning. They are effectively braised, but in an oven rather than on a hob. If you are already using the oven, it is a very easy way to ensure properly cooked vegetables.

Roasting

Most root vegetables roast well, although you must ensure that, when they go into the oven, both the oven and the fat are hot enough to crisp their outsides. It always pays to parboil them and to roughen the skin with a fork before putting them in the oven. This reduces cooking time and gives a better surface to crisp up. Any clean fat will do for roasting – lard, dripping, butter or oil, depending on what flavour you wish to impart to the vegetable. Make sure that you either baste the vegetables or roll them in the fat so that they get coated.

If the vegetables have failed to get crunchy by the time you need to serve them, finish them off under the grill. However, you will need to watch them like a hawk, as the fat assimilated into the vegetable will burn very easily.

Frying/sautéeing/deep-frying

As with all frying, the essential element in achieving perfection is hot, clean fat. Vegetables that have been partly or wholly boiled must be well drained and dried or they will never attain crispness. If the fat erupts into a seething inferno when you lower the vegetable in, take it out again, dry it with paper towel, toss it in seasoned flour and try again. If it merely boils soggily, the fat is not hot enough.

For deep-fried or frittered vegetables, the fritter batter should always be light. Flouring helps the batter to cling to the vegetable. If the batter coating is not crisp, return it to the fat even at the risk of marginally overcooking the inside – there is nothing worse than soggy batter surrounding soggy vegetable.

To deep-fry thin strips of any vegetable, including potatoes (i.e. chips), the fat must be really hot and clean, so that the outside seals before the fat can penetrate into the body of the vegetable making the whole thing leaden. Again, return the chip or whatever it is to the pan if the outside is not well crisped, even at the risk of slightly overcooking the inside. With potato chips it always pays to deep-fry them twice: the first time at a relatively low heat to cook the potato; the second time to brown and crisp.

If desperate, you can finish the vegetable off in a hot oven which will crisp the outside, but does have rather too drying an effect, so that the vegetable may end up by being not only crisp but dried out!

Frying or browning as a preliminary to braising or baking is an entirely different matter. The heat of the fat and the amount you fry the vegetable will depend on whether you need it crisped and brown or merely melted and softened.

Stir-frying

Stir-frying has only made its presence felt since the last war and is an excellent way to cook any 'light', 'slim' vegetable – Chinese leaves, beanshoots or any vegetable that has been cut into slender strips. To enjoy stir-fried cooking, you must like your vegetables crispy and slightly underdone – 'sog' lovers will have no time for them at all.

Successful stir-frying depends on very hot, light oil and a very hot pan. Cooking must be extremely speedy and you must have a hot serving dish ready for the vegetables. The only problem that can arise with stir-frying is if the vegetable pieces are not the same size, as there is no time for the thicker ones to cook through.

Vegetables with particular problems

Asparagus

The trick with asparagus is to keep the stems and tips in one piece while they cook. All too often the string holding the bunch is tied so tight that it slices through the sticks, cutting off the delicate tips. Success attends those who get the woody bottoms of the asparagus in boiling water but keep the heads merely in steam. If you have an asparagus saucepan, there is no problem. If not, use any kind of basket that fits in the saucepan – but whose handle you can still get at without burning your hand. Tie the asparagus sticks fairly loosely and stand them in the basket. Put a few inches/centimetres of water in the bottom of the pan, then cover the tips either with another saucepan that fits neatly over the bottom one or with foil tied over them like a hood but not touching them. With luck, once they are cooked, you will be able to lift out the basket, lay it on its side and cut the string without the tips falling off the asparagus. If you cannot lay your hands on a basket, stand the tied bunches upright in a saucepan as near their own size as possible. Cook as before, then drain the saucepan carefully by tipping it gently until you can get your hand in and remove the asparagus without breaking it.

If all fails and the sticks do come apart, lay them out on the plate and decorate the break with a little chopped parsley or the Hollandaise you were going to serve with them. You will have to give your guests a spoon or fork but, if your nerve holds, you could always suggest that this was the newest way of eating asparagus!

Aubergines (Eggplants)

Remember that an aubergine skin can be bitter so, unless you need it to keep the vegetable together (if the aubergines are to be stuffed), remove it. If you have time, pre-salt and drain the aubergines, as this does prevent them soaking up so much oil when you fry them.

Avocados

Provided they are ripe (and not over-ripe), avocados are totally trouble-free. Just make sure the dressing is sharp enough without being so sharp that it kills the flavour. If they are not to be used at once, remember to rub the cut surface with lemon juice or wine vinegar. If the surface does discolour, just before you serve them take a very thin slice off the top with a sharp knife.

If the avocados are overripe but the staining is not too bad, serve them with an opaque dressing or filling rather than a clear one so that their blemishes will not be so apparent – just a little cream, yoghurt or mayonnaise added to the dressing will do the trick. However, if they are really blackened, they will look horrible, even if the flavour is still good. In that case, you would do better to remove the flesh and mash it into a purée or mousse. Add cream, mayonnaise, cream cheese (although this is rather strong), lemon juice, a touch of tabasco, chopped black olives or tomatoes to turn it into a guacamole.

If, on the other hand, they are as hard as bullets . . . If you can get the flesh out of the shell keeping it intact, do so – you will then be able to serve the flesh in it. If you cannot, discard the shell, chop the avocado roughly and mix it with a filling: a rich, creamy béchamel with some blanched fennel, prawns, chopped chicken, Parmesan cheese, or anything that would blend reasonably well with the avocado. If the shells survived, pile the mixture into them; if not, put the mixture into ramekin dishes and either bake in the oven for 10 minutes or put under the grill for 3–4 minutes. If you had some frozen pancakes, you could also use the mixture to stuff them.

Broad beans

When young, broad beans can be cooked and eaten in their pods. When old, even the inner shell to the bean is tough. Either they should be shelled, which is a labour-intensive job and tends to leave you with rather battered beans, or they should be puréed.

Beetroot

Beetroot is one of the few vegetables that does need to be cooked in plenty of water, if it is to be cooked at all. Do not discard the water from the beets (or any other vegetable) – it makes wonderful soup! To serve it raw, cut into dice or matchsticks or grate it and mix with other vegetables, or serve on its own.

Brussels sprouts

Brussels sprouts benefit more than anything else from steaming rather than boiling. It is not necessary to cut the stems – it just makes them soggy in the middle.

Cabbages (and spring greens)

Cabbage has to be the most long-suffering vegetable in the annals of cooking and the most frequently ruined by sloshing around in buckets of water. To boil it, use very little water – preferably with some butter and maybe a little stock – and stop cooking when it is still crunchy. Alternatively, cook it long and slow in a peasant-type stew. Red cabbage is particularly good for this as it does not lose its crunchy nuttiness and it develops in flavour as it goes.

Overcooked cabbage is unredeemable and should go out. Undercooked cabbage can be cooked a *little* more. For flavour, add salted butter rather than salt.

Carrots

Carrots are pretty forgiving except when they are old and tough. At this point, they should be grated or diced very small. A little sugar also helps an elderly carrot. Undercooked carrots, as long as they are young, are delicious. Overcooked carrots should be puréed and mixed, if possible, with something like potato to give them a little more body. Toasted sunflower seeds scattered over the top add class.

Cauliflower

Always cook cauliflower in the minimum amount of water or steam it to keep the florets as perfect as possible.

If making a cauliflower cheese, do not make the sauce too thick – a light sauce through which the florets can poke is much more attractive to the eye and the palate. Soggy and overcooked cauliflower can only be puréed – and then only if you are desperate. Plenty of toasted flaked almonds or a layer of well-toasted brown breadcrumbs over the top could almost make it respectable again.

Celery

Celery is another sufferer from the buckets of water syndrome. Celery is best just lightly blanched and then braised in butter. However, you do need to get rid of the strings, which have an awful tendency to wedge themselves between guests' teeth. If they will not pull off, use a sharp knife to remove them. Really soggy celery would be best turned into soup but, if you have to use it, chop it as small as possible and mix it with puréed potatoes (if necessary, instant to which you have added lots of butter and cream) and top it with toasted flaked or crushed almonds, sunflower seeds, or something similar.

Leeks

Leeks, like cabbages, suffer greatly from sogginess. If overcooked, they really should only go into soup or form the base for a sauce. If you have time, mix them with some cheese and a béchamel sauce and turn them into a soufflé – but you will need to have patient guests! Leeks are best if braised or steamed and then served with butter. Take care with old leeks that you cut out all the woody centre, which is tasteless and rather unattractive.

Peppers

Pepper skins can taste bitter when boiled although when fried or braised, as for a ratatouille or pilaff, they are fine. They can be removed by burning under a grill and then washing off the blackened skin, or by submerging in hot oil and then peeling off the skin, as for a tomato, but both are fiddly processes.

There is really nothing you can do to counteract the bitterness of the pepper skins, which will penetrate endless layers of cream and sauce.

Potatoes

Problems with potatoes for most people stem not from what they do to them or how they cook them but from the fact that they have used the wrong type for the wrong dish. Greengrocers are reasonably helpful and mark different types; supermarkets are not at all and merely sell you a bag with no indication as to whether the potatoes are as waxy as candles or as floury as a bread bin.

As a very rough guide, young, early potatoes tend to be waxy and are therefore good for boiling or steaming, chipping or sautéeing, roasting or for salads. Maincrop potatoes, which are available from September onwards, are flourier and therefore much better for mashing and baking and more likely to disintegrate when you use them for salads.

Mashed potatoes made with waxy potatoes are problematic – even more so if you attempt to mash them in a food processor when they will turn into a grey liquid glue and are fit only for the dustbin. Any potato is better puréed with a ricer (a sort of garlic squeezer through which you press the vegetable), potato masher or *mouli-légume*; electric gadgets batter the texture of the vegetable out of existence. If you do have a disaster with waxy mashed potatoes and

achieve grey glue, abandon it. Make some instant potato with lots of butter, seasoning, cream and some chopped onions, dried mushrooms, chopped nuts, or anything to disguise its origins.

The same hazard occurs if you use waxy potatoes to make the sliced and baked dishes like pommes Anna. The potatoes will refuse to absorb the sauce as they should. Try taking them out, chopping the whole mixture roughly, adding a little more of whatever the liquid element was, and returning it to the oven. Depending on the texture of the potato, the extra chopping may be enough to allow them to absorb the necessary amount of liquid to cook. You could then finish them off under the grill.

If faced with the other alternative – boiled potatoes that disintegrate because they are too floury, you can only bow to fate and mash them. This is no disaster if you had only intended them as boiled potatoes in the first place. If they were to be sautéed, chop them and fry them in lumps – a cross between a potato cake and a hash brown.

If you were trying to make a salad, you will have to mix them with mayonnaise, chopped onions, chives, parsley, etc. and turn them into a potato mould. This can almost be an improvement, as long as it is well flavoured. If you set it in a mould and chill it well, you should be able to turn it out and decorate it.

For roast and baked potatoes, see under roasting and baking sections.

Spinach

Spinach is another sufferer from too much water. Like cabbage, it needs to be cooked in the least possible amount of liquid, usually what is left on the leaves after washing is quite enough. If in doubt, add masses of butter, as spinach can absorb almost endless quantities. Moreover, if given enough butter to feed off, it is difficult to overcook spinach as it gradually turns itself into a purée.

Frozen or tinned spinach is always recognizable as such and should only be used in sauces, soups or stuffings where it is well disguised by the other ingredients. The only exception is frozen leaf spinach which, if cooked with enough butter and spices, can be *almost* as good as fresh.

Swedes and turnips

Both swedes and turnips can get very soggy and waterlogged, especially when old. However, they do take a lot of cooking. The best method is to steam them long and slowly so that they get cooked through without getting sodden. If they do overcook, purée them, and gradually dry them out in a large flat pan with plenty of butter. But do watch them as they will burn very easily. Turnips are excellent roasted, but do not bake them, as they have amazingly tough skins.

Tomatoes

Tomatoes, like potatoes, only go wrong if you use the wrong kind for the wrong job. Hard northern tomatoes should really only be used raw, or for stuffing, grilling or frying; they will never mush down properly for a sauce. On the other hand, soft southern tomatoes will tend to mush once cooked. Your best bet is to turn the mush into a sauce as it will never reconstitute itself. You can purée the unmushable tomatoes but you are better advised to use Italian tinned tomatoes for any dish which requires a good cooked tomato flavour.

Vegetable marrow

If a marrow is to be used as a vegetable rather than being stuffed, remove the flesh and steam it. It is so watery already that any attempt to boil it is a guaranteed failure. If you intend to cover it with a sauce, do so at the last moment otherwise the marrow will continue to leak water and you will end up with floating floury pools. If you have already added the sauce, suck out the water with a bulb baster.

If the marrow is to be stuffed, use a rice-based stuffing rather than a breadcrumb one, as the rice absorbs the marrow's liquid better than the crumbs, which just go soggy.

Salads

The worst thing that can happen to a salad is that it should be made out of old, tired and flabby vegetables. As long as the vegetables are really fresh and crisp you are halfway to a success.

Most salad vegetables will revive if washed well in ice-cold water, dried and put in a fridge for a couple of hours. Some are better left to soak in water – radishes, for example, or celery which needs to have the bottoms of the stems cut off and to be left standing in a jug of chilled water. Watercress should be put upside down in a bowl of cold water in the fridge, as it drinks through its leaves.

Do not chop salad vegetables too small – leafy vegetables, like lettuce or spinach, bruise when you cut them and the bruised edge will soon turn slimy.

For visual and gastronomic effect, do not mix too many opposing colours or tastes. A green leafy salad with just some bright red pepper or some radishes scattered about looks (and tastes) much better than a muddled mixture of ten different colours. It often pays to actually arrange a salad in a bowl with the outside leaves forming an inner bowl or dish and the various chopped vegetables in the middle. Do not be afraid of adding fruit, nuts or seeds to salads, as they add colour and texture.

Do not dress a leafy salad in advance as it only makes it soggy. Cooked vegetable salads though (potatoes, artichokes, etc.) should be dressed when hot as the flavours of the dressing are absorbed much better by the vegetable when it is warm than when it is cold.

Do pay attention to the dressing for a salad. If you do not have a very inspiring range of vegetables, an interesting dressing can raise it quite above itself! You can afford to be quite adventurous with dressings – but it might be wise to serve the more bizarre ones with the salad rather than on it, so your guests can choose whether or not they wish to indulge in your latest gastronomic madness.

Do not dish up an old salad – the contents always look and taste tired. Even if the salad has been dressed, it will make a remarkably good soup so it does not need to be wasted.

If you are stuck, do not forget that many tinned vegetables mix well with fresh ones, especially in salads, and may give just that lift you need for your boring collection of lettuce, tomato and cucumber. Tinned artichoke hearts, tinned pimentos, sweet corn (in discreet amounts), asparagus, palm hearts, haricots verts, frozen peas (if you have to), olives, mushrooms, or even pickled beets, gherkins or capers, if you want something a bit stronger, would all add interest to a boring salad.

Desserts

A cook's attitude to desserts usually depends on how well she has her waistline under control. But, even for those to whom every spoonful of cream means another day on dry biscuits and water, it is useful to be able to produce a spectacular dessert on occasion. Especially if the rest of the meal has had a few hiccups. Of course there are those disgusting people who can work their way through untold quantities of chocolate gâteau, banana splits and marrons glacés without growing a centimetre, and for them an extensive range of gooey desserts is a basic necessity of life.

Although there are tricky areas of dessert making – I would strongly advise all disaster-prone cooks to steer well clear of anything that requires boiling sugar to 'a crack' or spinning it for decoration – it is possible to create a very impressive dessert with relatively little hassle.

Fruit-based desserts

Fresh fruit

Fruit is the most easily accessible of dessert dishes and, if you cannot face the thought of 'creating' a dessert, a splurge in a good fruit shop, especially in the summer, can solve your problem.

If you are going for fresh fruit alone, ensure that the fruits are ripe and beautiful specimens. Splash out on something exotic, whatever the time of year, not just apples and bananas. And do not detract from the exotic fruit by crowding it. A ripe, glowing nectarine served only with some warm (scented) water in a finger bowl to clean the fingers is the most perfect of all desserts.

It is nearly always possible to tell if dessert fruit is ripe as it will give very slightly to gentle pressure. You can hit trouble with hard skinned fruits like pomegranates or melons, so always buy one extra (or in the case of melons slightly more than you need) so you can try it yourself first.

Underripe fruit/fruit salad

If the fruit is too underripe to be served alone, make it into a fruit salad where its hardness will be at least partially disguised by being cut into bite size pieces. Fresh or frozen orange juice with a small splash of liqueur (almost any will do, although a crème de menthe would overpower the fruit) makes refreshing juice.

Do not cut the pieces too small or they will turn into mush, and, as with a vegetable salad, do not crowd in too many different colours and flavours. A salad of fresh pineapple, a little fresh grapefruit and redcurrants will look – and taste – much better than apples, oranges, bananas, redcurrants, pineapple, kiwi fruit, passion fruit and pomegranates all piled in together – and the latter would probably cost more!

Orange salad

Fruit salads can be made from just one fruit, such as the ever popular orange or caramelized orange salad. This is easy to make and refreshing to eat, especially after a heavy meal. However, it does pay to spend time segmenting rather than just slicing the fruit.

When you pour the caramel onto the oranges, which you will have to do when it is hot or you will not be able to do it at all, the caramel will harden as it touches the cold oranges. Do not worry, it will melt again as the juice works on the caramel. Just make sure that you make it at least an hour before you want to use it.

Overripe fruit

A fruit salad is also useful if the fruit that you have is slightly overripe. However, cutting the fruit up causes it to 'go over the top' much quicker than if it was kept whole, so a fruit salad made of overripe fruit must be eaten immediately. You might do better to turn it into a fool, mousse or soufflé.

Fools

Fruit fools are simplicity itself but, because they only consist of the puréed fruit, sugar and whipped cream, they can be a little bland. A squeeze of lemon juice will add sharpness which sets off the fruit.

Stewed fruit

Some fruits benefit from cooking. Winter fruits such as rhubarb or cooking apples really cannot do without. Stewing is the commonest and easiest way to cook such fruit. However, remember that if you want to keep the pieces whole rather than mushed, make a syrup of the sugar and water and place the fruit in it to cook, rather than throwing the fruit, sugar and water all in together.

Crumbles

Crumbles have a nasty tendency to sog because the crumble mixture sits directly on top of the fruit which goes on exuding liquid as it cooks. Always drain off as much juice as possible from the fruit before putting the crumble on top, then serve the juice separately as a sauce. If the top does get juice-logged, make a little extra crumble mixture, sprinkle a thin layer on top of the soggy stuff and put it under the grill for a couple of minutes. At least there will be a crisp top to the soggy crumble.

Fruit pies

(For pastry problems see chapter.)

As regards the insides of fruit pies, remember that the fruit shrinks to between half and one third its original bulk in cooking so, if you are using fresh fruit in a pie, pile it up really high in the dish and support the crust with a pie funnel or an upturned egg cup. Apples are particularly bad at this, so be prepared and have some extra fruit to serve with the pie.

Fruit tarts

Fruit tarts are easy and rewarding but you must bake the flan case beforehand or it will go irretrievably soggy with the juice from the fruit. Even if the case has been baked blind it is wise to paint it with egg white to seal it further.

Always 'arrange' the fruit in a tart as

it is on view – it is just as easy as piling it in. It also pays to glaze it with some jelly or strained jam.

Glazing is easy to do as long as you remember that the longer you go on boiling the jam the thicker it will become. As soon as it is hot enough to spoon easily, take it off the heat and spoon it over the fruit in a good thick layer. If the jam is left to boil, it will become like India rubber when it cools and you will need a pick to get through

it. If this happens, ditch it. You could take the fruit out and refill the case but it would be much quicker to give your guests ice cream.

Baked fruit

The only regularly baked fruits are apples and there is very little that even the most disaster-prone cook can do to them – apart from putting them in the microwave! They will explode covering the oven with puréed apple and leaving a flaccid, pale green skin lying limply in the bottom of the dish. If this happens, all you can do is scrape what you can off the sides of the oven and make an instant apple soufflé. Fold in some sugar and stiffly beaten egg whites and bake in a hot oven for 15 minutes.

Oven-baked apples may split if they have not had a cut made round them to allow for expansion, but are usually reformable into an acceptable shape – and at least the skin is crisp.

Summer pudding

Summer pudding is such a delicious seasonal dessert that anybody with good access to soft fruit will want to make it. However, the hazards of 'measling' and disintegration are to be guarded against.

Measling is caused by insufficient soaking of the bread in the fruit juices before is is used to line the bowl. Only the juices from the fruit soak through, which often leaves patches of dry bread. If this happens, you can coax more juice into the pudding around the measled patches after it is turned out, but it is not very satisfactory.

Disintegration is caused both by a failure to overlap the bread properly and a failure to weight it. The bread must be firmly overlapped all round the bowl with separate pieces in the bottom and over the top to hold the whole thing together. Incidentally, brown bread is just as good as white and gives a slightly crunchier texture.

The pudding must be heavily weighted – a minimum of 4 lb/2 kg for a reasonable size pudding – and left for 12–24 hours before being turned out. This compacts the fruit and bread which will

cling together in loving embrace.

If the pudding does fall apart, you would be wiser to serve it in individual portions with whipped cream as it is very difficult to stick together again.

Boiled or steamed puddings

Today very few people boil or steam puddings except at Christmas, which is a shame because a steamed pudding is light and not really very fattening. It is also simple to make as long as you mix it well and steam it long enough to get it really light.

Leaden puddings

If, perchance, you end up with a steamed pudding that resembles a bag of ballast, crumble it up and fry it quickly in some butter, then serve it with the sauce originally intended to go with it – at least it will be crisp ballast.

Unmoulding

The other hazard is that the pudding will refuse to come out of the bowl. Grease the bowl well with unsalted butter and you should be all right, but, to be sure, line the bowl with greased foil which can then be peeled off. If the pudding does fall apart, you may be able to reconstruct it and then pour over the sauce – which hopefully will cover the splits. Otherwise, serve it in the kitchen!

Christmas pudding

Christmas puddings tend to cling together reasonably well, but do take care flaming them. Warm the brandy

first in a ladle or small saucepan and then light it, held well away from anything that could catch light. You do not want to be like a friend of mine who one year cooked for a very grand Christmas house party in Scotland. She got so enthusiastic about the brandy that she set the butler alight, which set off the fire alarm and the automatic sprinkler system, not only putting out the Christmas pudding but deluging all the guests as well!

Brandy butter

It is laborious, but brandy butter is best of all if whipped by hand. If you do make it in an electric mixer, make sure that it is very well whipped, light and fluffy. Brandy butter that is recognizable as butter ought to go out – or be used for making crêpes suzettes. If you do fail, substitute whipped, sweetened cream flavoured with a good splash of brandy.

Baked puddings

Baked puddings cover not only the old-fashioned rice or bread-and-butter puddings but evergreen favourites such as crème caramel and crème brûlée.

Ingredients

A baked pudding is difficult to ruin unless you are mean with the ingredients, cook it too fast or overcook it. Plenty of cream, big raisins or sultanas and brown sugar will make any rice or bread-and-butter pudding taste good. A mixture of cream and milk in a crème caramel will take it into the luxury range.

Overcooking

If eggs are involved, as they are in virtually all baked puddings, they must be cooked slowly so that they do not boil, thus ruining the texture of the dessert. This is not so vital with a rice- or bread-based pudding where the texture of the custard is already disguised by the contents, but it is essential with a pure custard such as a crème caramel. If this is boiled, the eggs will curdle and toughen and the result will be quite unusable. Always cook a crème caramel in a *bain-marie*, which tempers and diffuses the heat.

If you cook one of the solider puddings to a cinder, it is better to take it out of the dish, cut it into squares and fry the squares in butter. Then sprinkle them liberally with brown sugar and serve them with lots of cream or home-made custard.

Disintegration

If you are concerned about the crème caramel falling asunder when you un-mould it – which, if it is properly cooked, it can do all too easily – don't. If you have baked it in an attractive dish, just serve it direct from the dish and spoon the caramel from the bottom. If it does fall apart, there is nothing you can do about it. However, if you do want to turn out the crème caramel, bake it in a dish that it almost fills. This means that it has less far to 'fall' as it is unmoulded and the shock to its system may not be enough to cause it to split.

Crème brûlée

Crème brûlée has to be one of the most trying of desserts, yet, when well made, it is delicious.

The crème presents no problem as it is merely a richer version of crème caramel and only needs to be cooked very slowly. However, achieving a thin, crisp and even layer of caramel on top has defeated even great chefs.

The secret is a salamander, which is what was used when the dish was invented in Cambridge. This is a portable grill or a plate of steel that can be heated to a very high temperature and placed immediately over a dish to grill or crisp the top of it. With a crème brûlée it can be brought into sufficiently close contact with the layer of sugar on top of the cream to melt and caramelize the sugar before the cream gets affected by the heat.

However, most people do not have salamanders and have to make do with grills or broilers that are seldom straight, cook unevenly and whose flame is too far away from the sugar to caramelize it before the cream starts to melt and boil. The result is a crème brûlée with thick layers of partially melted sugar on top, or heavily caramelized sugar with boiled cream below.

Although, in strict culinary terms, it is cheating, the best way for the disaster-prone to circumvent the problem is to make the tops separately and just lay them on the crème before it is served. To do this, cut out a piece of foil fractionally larger than the top of the dish or dishes in which you want to serve the dessert and grease it thoroughly. Turn up a very small edge or restraining wall around the outside of the foil, then spread a very even and reasonably thin layer of sugar over the foil and melt it under the grill till well caramelized. Try to ensure that your grill pan is absolutely flat or the melting sugar will all run to one side. Allow it to cool and then peel the caramel discs off the foil and place them on top of the cooked crème.

Meringues

Beating

The secret of meringues is to beat hell out of them. In the days before electric mixers this made for an energetic afternoon, but all that you need to do now is put up with the noise while the mixer does it for you.

Whether you choose the method which tells you to beat the egg whites on their own till very stiff and then whisk in the sugar, or the one which puts sugar and egg whites in together from the start, does not matter; you merely need to go on beating until they are as stiff as the Eiffel Tower. This may take up to 5 minutes even with an electric whisk. If you do not beat them long enough, they will not hold their shape and will be granular and crumbly. Break these failures up and use them in a gâteau.

Proportions/ingredients

The proportions for meringues always remain 2 oz/50g sugar to 1 standard egg white. More sugar will cause weeping; less will spoil the texture and make them tasteless. Brown or white sugar is equally acceptable, although you will get a grittier texture with brown. A spoonful of vinegar or lemon juice helps to stabilize the egg white and adds a welcome sharpness. Adding other ingredients such as powdered nuts should not affect the meringue as long as no more than 25 per cent of the mixture is non-meringue and the meringue is really stiff.

Damp sugar can also cause meringues to fail. The water in the sugar affects the egg whites and prevents them whisking properly. If you are at all worried, dry the sugar out in a very low oven before you use it. If it is too late, rescue is not possible. Abandon that batch and start again.

Cooking

Ordinary meringues should be dried out rather than cooked and therefore should be baked at a very low temperature. Cook them too fast and you get a burnt outside and a soggy inside. If you catch them in time, turn the oven right down and continue to dry them out. They will be perfectly alright but a bit caramelized! Alternatively, use them at once. The combination of crunchy outside and soggy inside is quite pleasant, but it loses its charm when the whole thing goes soggy.

Disintegrated meringues

If your meringues fall apart for whatever reason, do not despair. Turn them into meringue gâteau by piling the bits artistically up with lots of whipped cream and decorating it with fresh fruit. Some frozen or tinned fruits can be used but they must be dry so that they do not weep into the meringue or the cream. They should also be reasonably tart to counteract the sweetness of the meringue. However, do not confuse frozen raspberries with frozen Brussels sprouts, as did one Indian cook who had never met a Brussels sprout before and thought them pretty enough to decorate the gâteau!

Meringue pies

Lemon and other meringue-topped pies need a much softer meringue, so they should be cooked quickly at a high temperature so that the outside gets browned and crunchy and the inside remains soft. Remember that the filling of the pie will expand in the heat of the oven, so leave a reasonable amount of space for the meringue above the filling and below the lip or the whole thing will bubble all over the oven.

Baked Alaska

A baked Alaska is very spectacular, and easy to achieve as long as the temperatures of the ingredients are as opposed as possible. To avoid the ice cream melting into the meringue, totally encase the ice cream in the sponge cake and freeze the whole thing including the sponge.

Heat the oven as hot as it will go and beat the meringue till it is as stiff as a board. You can whisk it ahead of time as it will hold for a couple of hours. Then encase the cake, with its ice cream filling, completely in the meringue, leaving no gaps, and whip it speedily into the oven. By the time the meringue is cooked, the cake should just be thawed, but the heat should not have penetrated as far as the ice cream. If you fail and end up with a lake of flowing meringue cream, abandon it and serve your guests plain ice cream. If you succeed, either stick a sparklet in the top and light it, or a small silver or metal container of warmed brandy or other spirit that you can set alight. Your reputation will be made for life!

Cake-based desserts

Cream, fresh fruit, nuts or praline, and a generous hand with the brandy or liqueur bottle will improve nearly all cake-based desserts and make most of them quite delicious.

Amalgamation

Once you come to layer your gâteau, if it is to be served as such, remember that, no matter how good the cake, it can be dry when served as a dessert. So either cut it in very thin layers with a good layer of cream or fruit between each, or soak the layers in a liqueur or a fruit juice. If you have failed to do this, then serve the slices with an accompanying sauce. Go to town on the top layer as, if it looks sufficiently impressive, the base will be less noticed. If you do not want to use fruit or cream, a marbled glacé icing (see page 127) looks very effective.

Trifles, etc.

If making cake-based desserts such as tipsy cakes or trifles, it is even more important that the cake be well moistened with fruit juices, wines, sherry or brandy. Whether or not you add fruit to the trifle, it is also essential that you use home-made or a good quality crème pâtissière or custard. If you cannot face the thought or making your own, most good supermarkets and delicatessens sell good fresh custards, but do not use a 'packet' as it is totally undisguisable.

Custards and sweet sauces

The most used and most abused of the sweet sauces is an egg custard; either what is unattractively called a 'boiled custard' (which is exactly what it should not be), or a crème pâtissière, which sounds harder, but is easier to achieve.

Boiled custard

A real crème anglaise or boiled custard, served instead of cream, is delicious but it is easy to curdle (since it depends only on egg yolks to thicken it) and it cannot be replaced with a packet — sweet packet sauces have a quite unmistakable 'packet' flavour. As with all egg sauces, the trick is never to boil the mixture. If it threatens to curdle, plunge the bowl into cold water, or tip the contents into a cold, clean bowl, and whisk until your arm falls off! You can insure against curdling by beating a teaspoonful of cornflour or cornstarch into the egg yolks before adding the milk, but the texture will suffer. If the sauce curdles beyond retrieval, your only hope is to blend it, which will help, and then maybe add some chopped almonds or toasted sesame seeds to disguise the granular texture.

Crème pâtissière

A crème pâtissière is easier to make as it involves flour or cornflour from the start. It is, however, very easy to lump! In the hopes of keeping it smooth, mix the flour very well into the egg yolks before adding the milk, scald the milk first (but let it cool slightly before

adding it so that it does not cook the eggs before you want it to) and add it very gradually, stirring continuously. If, despite your best endeavours, the crème still goes lumpy, cook it for a few minutes in the hope that the lumps will disperse, then whisk it with a balloon whisk. If the lumps still remain recalcitrant, put the crème through a sieve. Most important, stay with it throughout the process – turn your back for a moment and it will guaranteeably turn itself into sticky yellow boulders rolling around the bottom of your pan.

Chocolate sauce

Most modern cooking chocolate has never come within shouting distance of a cocoa nib and is therefore fairly indestructible. However, all chocolate, genuine or ersatz, burns easily, so always melt it over hot water rather than direct heat. Real chocolate sometimes stiffens after it has melted – in this case remove it from the heat and gradually stir in either a couple of tablespoonfuls of hot water, or a knob of melted butter. To safeguard against the stiffening, add the water or butter to the chocolate before you start to melt it. Occasionally, if overheated, chocolate will also go granular. Treat it as though it has stiffened and it may come back – or may not! If not, there is not much you can do about it. Either keep that lot to go in a soufflé or something where the texture does not matter and start again, or add a little bit of dark brown sugar to the sauce just before you serve it, so that the granular texture of the chocolate becomes an unusual feature rather than an eyesore!

To achieve a really good chocolaty flavour, you do have to cook the chocolate with the butter and water for 15–20 minutes. A spoonful of instant coffee is a great help. Instant drinking chocolate will never give the same flavour to a sauce as real chocolate but, if cooked long and strong enough, preferably with a little cocoa and instant coffee, it will be passable. Take care though as it is very sweet and you are unlikely to need any more sugar.

Fruit sauces

These are hard to damage unless you boil them dry. Even then they can usually be rescued by gradually adding water over a gentle heat and coaxing them back to life. If you want to get rid of seeds from the berry-type sauces, you will always have to sieve after blending as no liquidizer or food processor will break them up. Jam sauces are also hard to damage, except by overcooking. Do remember that they solidify as they cook, so that a thick, hot jam sauce will be like rubber when it cools. Again, gently add water to reduce the sauce to the right consistency.

Wine and egg sauces – champagne, sabayon, etc.

These are not 'hostess friendly' as they require last minute whisking over hot water if they are to retain their fluffiness. However, as with all other egg sauces, a pinch of arrowroot (which thickens at a lower temperature than the other flours) beaten with the egg and sugar before the wine is added will help it to hold its consistency.

Caramel

This is such a useful decoration that you should not allow yourself to be scared of it – especially since it is very simple. However, take care with it as it is *very hot* and can burn both people and things badly and easily.

Whether you melt the sugar by itself over the heat, or whether you add water from the beginning, does not matter. You need merely to ensure that the sugar melts and caramelizes fairly evenly. If one side is browning before the other has melted, turn down the heat and stir it well to amalgamate the two parts.

Very occasionally, the sugar will turn into crystals rather than melt and caramelize. This can be caused either by a defect in the refining of the sugar, or by contact with some sorts of nonstick surfaces. To be on the safe side, do not attempt to make caramel in nonstick pans. If it does crystallize, there is nothing you can do but throw it out and start again.

When the sugar has caramelized, if you wish to reduce it with water, take great care to stand well back when you add the water and add it very slowly. The caramel is so hot that it causes the water to vaporize instantly creating steam which can scald you badly. (For treatment of burns see page 14.)

If the caramel stiffens before you have done what you want with it, heat it up again very gently and it will liquify. Take care not to heat it too long or it will continue to cook and brown.

Praline

Praline is only whole almonds cooked in caramel, cooled and broken up and it is so useful as emergency decoration that

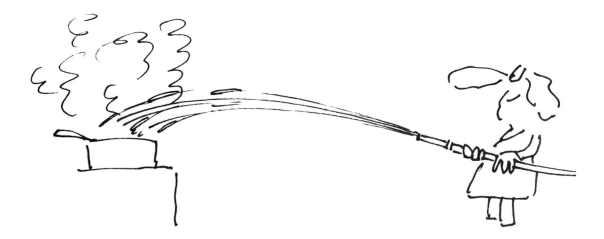

it is worth keeping some in stock. Provided that the jar in which it is stored is absolutely air and damp tight, it should keep for a couple of months. If it has gone soggy and glued itself together, *if* you can get it out of the container, melt it down again, cool it and recrush it.

Fresh cream

Although normally quite amenable, fresh cream is affected by the weather – for example, it hates humidity and will turn itself into butter with a couple of stirs on a really humid day.

Always keep fresh cream in the fridge, both to keep it fresh and because it whisks better if it is well chilled. The thinner the cream the more this applies, so that whipping cream should only ever be whisked just out of the fridge; single or coffee cream will not whip, no matter how cold.

If you have the time and energy, double cream, like egg whites, is better whisked by hand with a balloon whisk. The air is more evenly and lightly incorporated into the whole.

Always stop whipping as soon as the cream has reached soft peaks, very soon after that it will turn to butter. If it does, you can sometimes retrieve it by *very* gently stirring in some unwhipped or single cream. If not, put it in the middle of the gâteau or cake where it will not be noticed or keep it for cooking.

Never fold cream into a hot mixture. Whereas egg whites do not lose their texture when in contact with heat, cream melts.

Remember that slightly sour cream is a delicacy in France so do not throw out cream that has just turned. Make a feature of it by serving it sprinkled with sugar. Really sour cream is very bitter and should be thrown out.

Ice cream and sorbets

Even without an ice cream maker, home-made ice creams are easy and invaluable as standbys in times of crisis.

Ice cream makers are useful, as the constant motion of the paddle prevents ice crystals forming, particularly in sorbets, and creating a crystalline texture. However, the addition of extra egg yolks to give a creamier texture and vigorous whisking of the mixture before its final freezing will achieve almost the same result with a cream ice cream. Sorbets are more dificult, as there is so much greater a proportion of water in them. However, a good stir every 15 minutes or so until they are too stiff to stir any more should banish most of the crystals.

Do remember that too much sugar or too much alcohol will prevent the ice cream freezing properly. One part sugar to every four parts of liquid is as much sugar as it can stand. Since alcohol's freezing temperature is a great deal lower than that of water, one part alcohol to about six parts liquid would be the absolute maximum. Of course, if you want a really alcoholic sorbet, there is nothing to stop you serving it in glasses and allowing your guests to drink it.

Baking

Bread

Bread, being about the first thing that man made, is also about the easiest. Ordinary bread is only flour, salt, liquid and yeast, well kneaded to mix, and baked. The modern cook with a food processor need not even bother about the kneading (which is only done to spread the yeast really thoroughly through the bread) as the food processor does it all for her. Unless, of course, she enjoys doing battle with balls of dough!

Ingredients/yeast

Flours differ but, as long as the flour is of good quality and dry, the differences are a matter of personal taste. Water is the normal mixing liquid and sea salt has a better flavour than table salt.

If the yeast is fresh and alive, when put in a damp, warm atmosphere, it will rise and grow whether it is incorporated in a dough or alone. Old age kills both compressed and dried yeast, as do extremes of temperature: anything over 110°F/50°C or below standard refrigerator temperature.

Once the yeast has been creamed by mixing it with sugar and a little warm liquid, it needs only to be thoroughly amalgamated into the dough, by hand or machine.

Rising, etc.

After the yeast has been mixed in, the dough must be left to rise, and in some cases prove. This will happen more or less quickly depending on the ambient temperature, but the longer it takes, the better the bread will be. Elizabeth David, among others, maintains that bread that has been left for 24 hours in a moderately warm kitchen will taste far better than bread that has been 'hurried' in a warming oven. However, an hour should be the minimum time – unless you are using a food processor and extra vitamin C to assist the raising.

If the dough does not rise, it means that the yeast is dead – whether through old age or overheating – and there is nothing you can do about it. Dead yeast has a smell and flavour not unlike dead cats and is totally unrevivable. Throw it out and start again.

Once you have mastered the basic techniques of bread making, all fancy breads are merely an elaboration on them. Most bakery books are extremely explicit in their instructions.

Cakes

Raising agents

Most cakes use eggs or chemical raising agents rather than yeast. The lighter sponges use whisked egg white; heavier sponges or fruit cakes use whole eggs or a combination of whole eggs and baking powder or bicarbonate of soda. These work by giving off gases when heated, thereby raising the mixture. The more chemical raising agent one uses, the lighter, dryer and less keeping the cake will be. Thus, fresh light sponges or angel cakes should be eaten within 24 hours to be at their best; a rich Madeira cake will keep several weeks; a fruit cake several months.

Mixing

The early mixing processes in all cake making are important, be it beating eggs and sugar to a ribbon or creaming butter and sugar for Victoria sponges. In both cases, early and thorough beating ensures that the cake will remain moist. Beating later in the process when the flour has been added will make the cake tough, heavy and elastic. Obviously,

beating a light sponge after the egg white has been folded in would defeat the purpose of the operation.

For cakes that need to hold a filling in place – such as a cherry Madeira where you are attempting to keep the cherries in suspension – do not add all the liquid until you are sure that the full amount will not make the mixture too liquid to support the fruit.

Packet mixtures

If you feel that you cannot face the traumas of total cake making, there are a great number of excellent packet cake mixes on the market and you might be well advised to give up the whole business of being a home baker and use one of them.

Cooking

Follow the instructions in the recipe (or on the packet) for baking times and temperatures but do check yourself, as your oven may not behave exactly as the instructions say it should. Do not, however, continually open and shut the oven, as you will kill whatever chance the poor thing had of rising evenly in a constant heat. Similarly, when you test it, do not be too vigorous. If a light sponge gets a fat skewer stuck in it, it will break the crust and release half the air being carefully husbanded inside. Press the sponge very gently with your finger and, if it resists, it will be done. A more robust cake will stand the skewer treatment but, even then, do not do it more than you must.

Turning out

Whether the mixture is from a packet or home-made, it is most important that you are able to get it out of the tin when it is cooked. Greasing and flouring tins *should* work but has been known, only too often, not to – especially if the butter was salty! Invest in one, or several, loose-bottomed cake tins, which guarantee complete success – not only for cakes but for pâtés, mousses, jellies or anything else that you fear may lurk shyly in its container and refuse to emerge in public. If the mixture is very liquid, as in a very light sponge, line the tin with greaseproof paper to prevent it leaking out the bottom.

Swiss roll

If you are making a Swiss roll, then line the tin with greaseproof paper, but do ensure that you grease the paper well before pouring in the mixture. Try also to ensure that the oven shelf is level or all the mixture will run to one side. If it does, all is not lost, although it will be rather difficult to roll. When you turn the Swiss roll out, do so onto a tea cloth or piece of greaseproof paper that has been coated well with icing sugar. If not well sugared, the Swiss roll will stick to the cloth or paper and you will have a terrible time rolling it. If you have not greased the paper properly, you will also have a terrible time peeling it off, but patience will usually win the day. Do not worry if the roll is not entirely perfect. As long as you can keep about one third of it intact, that will do for the outside and no one will see the inside. Dredge it thoroughly with sugar or icing sugar. Or, if it has really fallen apart, pre-slice it before serving so that no one can see.

Failed sponge cake

If, despite your best endeavours, your sponge cake, be it light or rich, is dry, crumbly, flat, lumpy or generally unappealing, do not throw it out. If you are desperate for a complete cake or dessert, cut the sponge into *very* thin layers, sprinkle each with a little liqueur if for a dessert, and layer *very* generously with filling so that the cake gets smothered. Then top or ice equally generously and no one will ever know. If you do not need the cake too urgently, keep it to make trifles, tipsy cakes or anything that needs a sponge base. Buried deep enough and soaked comprehensively enough, even the most revolting cake will become quite palatable. Alternatively, crumble it and use it as a topping. When toasted, the crumbs can be used as decoration for almost anything in need of disguise.

This does not apply only to plain sponges. Orange or lemon sponges would be a delicious base for any cream dessert, chocolate, coffee or even gingerbread can be used as a base for 'a trifle with a difference'. Indeed, coffee and chocolate cake could be sliced into fingers, thoroughly dried out in the oven and sandwiched together with some butter icing as biscuits. Any of the above could be used as the base for a baked pudding, but remember that the cake will be sweeter than bread or rice so reduce the amount of sugar.

Failed fruit cakes

Failed fruit cakes are just as adaptable.

Rich fruit cakes often get old and dry out. Do not abandon them to the birds. Cut deep slits in the top of the cake and feed with a mixture of brandy and sherry, or, if you do not want to be too alcoholic, a fruit wine or good fruit cordial. The amount you give the cake will depend on how dry it is, but you can always cut it in half and test the middle.

The same principle can be applied to lighter fruit cakes although one needs to be more temperate. A large quantity of fruit will soak up the liquid and make the whole mixture moist but sponge will merely become soggy, so the greater the proportion of sponge to fruit the less liquid it should be given. It is usually better to ice the cake after it has been 'fed' – to conceal the tell tale signs.

If a rich fruit cake really is dry beyond redemption, break it up in a bowl, add some suet and a goodly measure of liquor, leave it to soak for 24 hours, then squash it well into a bowl and steam it as a Christmas pudding. It will be a little crumbly and somewhat lighter than the standard, but many people prefer it that way!

Icings

The disaster-prone cook should steer clear of all but glacé, butter and royal icing – fondants and their kind are for those with time and expertise to spare.

Glacé icing

Glacé icing is quick and simple but messy. It is not easy to get the proportion of icing sugar to liquid right to achieve 'spreadability' without 'runability'.

Always put whatever you are going to ice on a rack so that the extra can run off without getting stuck in a thick frill round the bottom of the cake. Arm yourself with a pot of boiling water and several metal spatulas or flat knives to smooth out the lumps. Inevitably, the wretched stuff will never quite cover the top of the cake in the first run, and when you add the next bit, the first will have dried and the whole thing will go lumpy. Only practice is going to perfect your technique, but smoothing with a spatula dipped in boiling water does help.

Always be ready to decorate or disguise the top with something other than icing – even if only gold and silver balls. Grated chocolate is a good alternative.

Marbling

Marbling the top, if it is reasonable, will distract the eye from any minor blemishes and is easy and impressive in itself. Run a little melted chocolate, or different coloured icing, in parallel lines across the top of the cake. Then, before it is dried, take a knife point and pull it across the cake top in straight lines at right angles to the first lines, thus pulling the lines into a feathered shape. Try it a couple of times on greaseproof paper before you launch into the cake.

If all fails and you make a complete mess of the icing, wait till it is dry, then scrape the whole lot off and start again.

Butter icing

Butter icing is the world's easiest, but it is very rich. Many people prefer to use shortening as the fat base, which keeps it much lighter. The only hazard with butter icing is to get enough flavour into it. Like brandy butter (which is, of course, only a butter icing) nothing is nastier than a butter icing that tastes like sweetened butter. Therefore, taste after you have followed the recipe. If you have used a particularly strongly flavoured butter, you will need more chocolate, lemon or whatever you are using. Never try to spread it straight out of the fridge.

Royal icing

Royal icing is also simple, using egg white rather than water or syrup to moisten the icing sugar. Add a little lemon juice to counteract the sweetness and do not forget a drop or two of glycerine to prevent it hardening totally. If you do have a cake with unglycerined icing, you would be better advised to saw your way through it with a bread knife rather than to try and cut it, when it will shatter and ricochet all over the drawing room and Great Aunt Ethel. Royal icing can always be broken off and replaced with a new batch. Use a small amount of icing to experiment with the colour.

Marzipan

It pays to make your own marzipan as the real thing tastes so much better than bought. Since it is only a question of beating together ground almonds, sugar and egg white to moisten, there is nothing to go wrong.

Biscuits

Biscuits are simple to make and home-made biscuits always impress guests.

They have four dangers: being too soft so that they spread into shapeless plops; being too short or having too great a proportion of fat which makes them hopelessly crumbly; being overhandled, like pastry, which makes them tough;

and getting overcooked, which they will do at the drop of a hat.

Texture

Since most biscuit mixtures contain butter, they will always become softer when they go in the oven, so, if your mixture is very runny when cold, it will run away altogether once it gets hot. Unless the mixture is being cooked in a restraining tin try to ensure a reasonably firm texture. Apart from anything else, if it is too runny the biscuit will tend to be tough.

Crumbling

If you want to use a very short mixture, mould the dough by hand rather than trying to roll it out, as you will not succeed. Cut the biscuits into fat rather than thin shapes so they have more chance of holding together.

Toughness

Do not handle the biscuits more than necessary to get the ingredients well mixed.

Overcooking

Once the biscuits have gone in the oven, watch them like a hawk. Take one out and cool it to test, as a biscuit, especially a dark coloured one such as chocolate or ginger, will often be cooked long before it looks cooked.

Failures

Biscuits that have fallen apart, spread or generally failed to live up to expectations, can always be broken up and used as decorations, or crumbled and used as biscuit bases (held together with butter or egg white) for dishes such as cheesecakes.

Recipes to the Rescue

Hors d'oeuvre

Devilled nuts

Any selection of whole or broken nuts, as diverse as possible, lightly fried in a little oil and sprinkled with sea salt and cayenne pepper.

Crudités

Any selection of raw vegetables, cut into finger-size pieces; as many different shapes and colours as you can manage. Arrange them on a dish and serve with a bowl of dip.

Dips

Yoghurt, crushed clove of garlic, lemon juice and salt.

Cream cheese and chives/chopped peppers/tabasco, etc.

Any decent chutney/pickle with a little whipped cream.

Mayonnaise – straight/with curry paste/ anchovy essence or fillets/mustard – French, whole grain, etc.

Spinach consommé × 4

8 oz/225 g frozen or 1 14 oz/397 g can puréed spinach
2 14 oz/397 g cans good consommé

Mix them together and heat with a splash of sherry, salt, pepper and nutmeg.

Grilled grapefruit

½ grapefruit per person, sectioned, sprinkled with dark brown sugar and frizzled under a hot grill for a couple of minutes.

Prawn cocktail

2 oz/50 g frozen, thawed prawns per person
2 fl oz/60 ml double cream/yoghurt per person

Lightly whisk cream and add tomato purée, salt, pepper and lemon juice to taste. Serve prawns plus sauce on anything green and leafy.

Vegetables au gratin

Any tinned or frozen 'smart' vegetable – asparagus, artichoke hearts, palm hearts, etc., drained and laid on brown toast. Sprinkle with grated cheese, brown under the grill and finish with freshly ground black pepper.

Baked eggs

Line the bottom of ramekin dishes with slices of skinned tomato, a little frozen spinach or asparagus tips, etc. – or any combination. Break the egg over the top and spoon over a little cream, fresh or slightly sour, lightly seasoned and flavoured with a little tomato purée, mild cheese, etc. Bake approximately 10 minutes in a moderate oven till set.

Main courses

Pancake cake

Frozen pancakes (approximately 3 per person) layered with vegetables (spinach, chopped and drained/ tomatoes, well drained if tinned/ asparagus/mashed green peas, etc.), fish (tinned tuna, prawns, etc.) or meat, but not the chewy kinds – tongue or paté are fine.

Cover with an instant sauce or cream and sprinkle with a little grated cheese. Warm through in an oven or microwave and finish off under the grill.

Risotto

Frozen rice (approximately 4 oz/100 g/½ cup per person) with a few onions lightly fried in butter, tinned or frozen vegetables (mushrooms, corn, green peas, artichoke hearts, etc.) and tinned or frozen fish (tuna, prawns, mussels, cockles, etc.). Add chopped olives, capers, nuts, etc. Add liquid from cans with white wine and/or lemon juice and plenty of seasoning and herbs.

Fish platter

A good selection of frozen and/or good tinned fish: crab claws, large prawns, cockles, mussels, smoked salmon, smoked trout or smoked mackerel, little cooked white fish, squid, sardines, etc. Arrange everything on a dish (well thawed!) with some mayonnaise – home-made, if available, or bought disguised with a little lemon juice, garlic, tabasco, etc. Serve with fresh (frozen . . .) bread.

Calves' liver

Calves' liver out of freezer lightly fried in a little butter, with cream (fresh or slightly sour), frizzled bacon pieces, fresh or tinned mushrooms and brandy.

Or, lightly fried in butter with bacon and fresh apple rings – preferably cooking apples.

Sauces

Instant brown sauce

To smarten up frozen brown sauce, add cherries/finely sliced orange rind and juice/prunes, chopped/brandy, port, etc.

Instant tomato sauce

Mash a can of tomatoes with some tomato purée, dried onions and herbs, salt and pepper and cook for 5 minutes. Greatly improved if you also add some garlic, bacon pieces, white wine and/or cream.

Instant cream sauce

Fresh or slightly sour cream with lemon juice, fresh or dried chopped herbs and seasoning.

Vegetables

Any frozen or tinned vegetables can be smartened up by sprinkling over chopped nuts, seeds or grated cheese. Frozen or tinned vegetables can be disguised by being puréed and mixed with instant potato – well seasoned with salt, pepper and 'appropriate' herbs, sprinkled generously with cheese or breadcrumbs and browned under the grill.

Classier tinned and frozen vegetables can be made into good salads by being dressed (while warm if possible) and then sprinkled with nuts, seeds or crushed hard-boiled egg yolk.

Desserts

Crèpes suzette x4

8 frozen pancakes.
If possible use pre-frozen sauce for crèpes suzettes (which keeps excellently). Otherwise, make an instant sauce with the rind of 2 oranges scraped onto 2 lumps of sugar, then mix the sugar with the juice of the oranges, 2 oz/50 g butter (unsalted if you have it) and 2 tablespoons of an orange based liqueur – preferably all done in front of guests to impress them. Warm the pancakes in the sauce, fold them, add 2 tablespoons warmed brandy, and set light to the sauce.

Ice cream pancakes

Fill frozen (thawed) pancakes with a block of good ice cream or fresh or frozen fruit, and cover the whole thing with a sauce made of heated jam.

Ice creams

Home-made or good quality ice cream served with liqueurs (coffee ice cream and Tia Maria/chocolate or vanilla with crème de menthe, etc.), nuts or seeds, or fresh or frozen fruits – or a combination of the lot!

Sponge gâteau

A shop bought sponge base (or a home-made frozen sponge base/cake) sprinkled generously with a fruit liqueur, covered with tinned or frozen fruit and whipped cream, plain, sweetened, or flavoured with the liqueur.

Lychees

Tinned lychees with a little strong china tea added to their juice.

Meringues

Combine them with good ice cream, cream, or fresh or good frozen fruits.

Emergency Equipment and Food Supplies

BATTERIE DE CUISINE

loose-bottomed cake
tins of various sizes
and shapes
bulb baster
fat separator jug
flat metal 'sieve' (for
draining excess
liquid)
large flat metal plate
or tray
a very wide fish slice
flexible palate knives
of various sizes
skimmer
a good vegetable peeler
a puréer of some kind –
electric or hand
a microwave, if
possible, (for
defrosting
emergency rations!)

FOOD SUPPLIES

Fresh goods
double cream
spare milk
spare butter
plenty of eggs
bacon
lumpfish roe
good olives, stuffed or
plain
cheese, both as
emergency course
and for 'improving'
something
onions – all types
lemons and oranges

parsley
radishes
garlic
fresh ginger root
red and white cabbage

Dried goods
pastas – various
rices – various
instant potato
potato crisps
dried onions and
mushrooms
assorted seeds – poppy,
sunflower, sesame,
caraway, etc.
nuts of all kinds –
especially almonds,
toasted and
untoasted
tomato purée – tube or
tin
assorted packet sauces
chicken and beef stock
cubes
good selection dried
herbs
good selection spices
plenty of gelatine
aspic
meat and vegetable
extracts
salted peanuts
unusual cheese
biscuits
olive oil
wine and cider vinegar
dried fruits – raisins,
figs, prunes, etc.
maraschino cherries
dark brown sugar

cooking and dessert
chocolate
packet sponge bases
meringues
assorted good jams and
preserves
praline
candied or crystallized
flowers or fruits

Tinned goods
assorted soups and
consommés
tinned pâté – good
quality
anchovies, tuna fish
and assorted fish
stewed steak in gravy
plum tomatoes
various vegetables,
exotic and other –
celery hearts, palm
hearts, artichoke
hearts, asparagus,
mushrooms, etc.
assorted beans
fruits preserved in
liqueurs
exotic tinned fruits

Frozen goods
gourmet and cooking
cheese
bacon
good quality steaks
assorted 'glamorous'
shellfish
various casseroles
pancakes
cooked rice (for
emergency
vegetable)

good selection of
vegetables
fresh pastas
selection of frozen
fresh herbs
home-made soups
home-made sauces
butter based pâtés –
kipper, etc.
various uncooked
pastries
good brown or white
bread
garlic or herb breads
and butters
orange juice
home-made or bought
ice creams
frozen raspberries,
loganberries, etc.
chocolate mints

Liquor
brandy
sherries – various
assorted liqueurs
red and white wine –
for cooking

Sauces
horseradish
various interesting
mustards
good or home-made
pickles and chutneys
Worcestershire sauce
curry pastes
soya sauce
tomato ketchup
mayonnaise
assorted packet sauces

Index

Page numbers in italics indicate illustrations